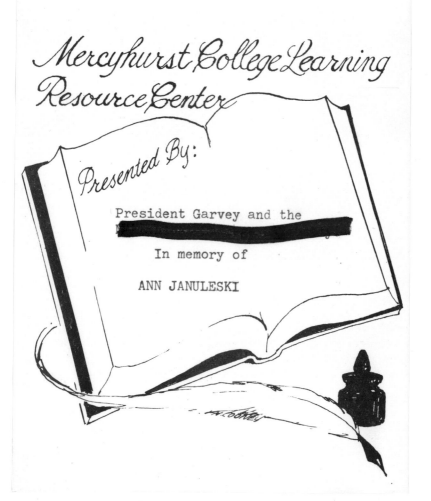

Mercyhurst College Learning Resource Center

Presented By:

President Garvey and the ▬▬▬▬▬▬▬▬▬▬

In memory of

ANN JANULESKI

the formation of the polish state

the formation of the polish state

The Period of Ducal Rule
963–1194

by Tadeusz Manteuffel
Translated and with an
Introduction
by Andrew Gorski

Wayne State University Press
Detroit, 1982

Originally published as "Polska w okresie
prawa książęcego, 963–1194," *Historyk wobec
historii* (Warsaw: Państwowe Wydawnictwo
Naukowe, 1976), pp. 122–264. English
translation copyright © 1982 by Wayne State
University Press, Detroit, Michigan 48202.

Library of Congress Cataloging in Publication Data
Manteuffel, Tadeusz, 1902–1970.
The formation of the Polish state.

Translation, with minor changes, of: "Polska
w okresie prawa książęcego, 963–1194,"
published in 1976 in the author's Historyk
wobec historii, p. 122–263
Includes bibliographical references and index.
1. Poland—History—Piast period, 960-1368.
I. Gorski, Andrew. II. Title.
DK4212.M3613   943.8'02   81-11583
ISBN 0-8143-1682-4   AACR2

Publication of this book has been supported
in part by a grant from the Polish Studies
Program of Wayne State University.

Contents

Foreword

One of the favorite images of intellectuals in those Middle Ages that Professor Tadeusz Manteuffel studied so sensitively and thoroughly was one attributed to the great twelfth-century teacher Bernard of Chartres. He used to say, so one of his students reports to us, that "we were like dwarfs seated on the shoulders of giants. If we see more and further than they, it is not due to our own clear eyes or tall bodies, but because we are raised on high and upborne by their gigantic bigness." Tadeusz Manteuffel was such a giant, and a legion of students, colleagues, and friends stand gladly upon his shoulders. We are better scholars than we could otherwise be on our own, and we are better people because we are uplifted by the example of his personal integrity. It is therefore a distinct pleasure, by way of providing the Foreword to this fine translation of one of Manteuffel's most useful works, to say something about him as a person, about his historiographical importance, and about the significance of the subject of the book before us.

Tadeusz Manteuffel was an imposing personality. His craggy and stern visage, the intensity of his questions and conversation, and the massive eyebrows which shadowed his deep-set eyes combined to make one's first meeting with him an unsettling experience. But there was far more to the man than this impressive exterior, as a personal anecdote may illustrate.

With my wife and two infant children, I arrived in Warsaw for the first time in the summer of 1966. Recently completed doctoral study had introduced me to the wonders of Polish history and culture, while instruction in the language had been sufficient to develop a reading knowledge of historical writing. A rather formal and traditional approach to grammar and literature, however, had left me woefully unprepared to cope with the complexities of living in Poland. (Being able to declaim in Polish "Woe betide the hares!" was useful in pursuing the study of Mickiewicz's literary evocation of the "last hunt" in eighteenth-century Lithuania, but it was not of much help in finding an apartment and making sure we had groceries to eat.) Equally troublesome was the fact that in my naiveté, I had come to Poland without official sponsorship and attachment to any institute or university center. Neither had I had contact with Polish scholars. All I had was the suggestion from the director of my graduate work that I contact Professor Manteuffel in Warsaw. After much frustrating trial and error, I was able to do this.

When the secretary at the Academy of Sciences' Institute of History ushered me into the director's office on the old town square, she could scarcely have known the extent of my trepidation. I was unsure of the language, unsettled by the realities of coping with life in contemporary eastern Europe, and apprehensive about meeting the dean of Polish medievalists. The dim interior of the room, lit in the waning afternoon only by exterior light, did little to bolster my spirits; Manteuffel's initially rather brusque and formal questions ("Who are you?" "What is your preparation?" "What do you wish to do here in Poland?") served almost to convince me that I had made a mistake in ever taking up the study of Polish medieval history. Eventually, he inquired how I had come to contact him. When I mentioned my mentor's recommendation, a palpable air of tenseness and formality sublimed almost immediately into an atmosphere of discursive reflection. He stared into the distance and remembered my American Professor, with whom he had been able to keep in contact in the preceding two decades. He described him as one who "had been very helpful during some difficult times."

Manteuffel went on to question me in detail about my interest in the foreign policy of King Casimir the Great. What he asked was probing, but not hostile; he treated me as a junior colleague, though his knowledge was far deeper and broader than mine. His

questions themselves were informative and stimulating. Then he
began to talk about the issues related to the problem of feudalism
and about the article he had sent to the American journal *Medievalia et Humanistica* on this subject. (He did not know I had read
his Polish typescript two years before, while helping the editor
prepare an English translation for publication.) From there, Manteuffel moved to a discussion—part lecture, part conversation—of
the course of Polish historiography in the past twenty years. He
compared it with prewar writing, placed it within the context of
European intellectual and political traditions, and suggested what
directions it was liable to take in subsequent years. Finally, he
called in the secretary to dictate letters of introduction for me to
libraries, archives, and people in Warsaw and Kraków, my ulti-
mate destination on that trip. In these two hours, the formal
representative of Polish academic and historical institutions had
become the teacher and nestor for one who needed guidance and
orientation. It was in these moments I first learned something of
the skill and wisdom and integrity of the individual who was the
doyen of Polish medievalists in the era between Marceli Handelsman and Aleksander Gieysztor.

My experience was, in many respects, a microcosm of the
larger universe of relationships others had with Manteuffel. He
was a somewhat formal individual in the tradition of European
professors. Only with close friends of long standing was he re-
laxed. In addition, he was a very intense individual, particularly
with regard to his scholarship and teaching. This allowed him to
speak with the authority of one who had gone "to the sources"
and mastered them. His peers and his students remember him as
one to whom they always turned for guidance and enlightenment.
They were never disappointed, for, just as with me, he was un-
sparing in sharing the fruits of his learning. The intellectual
breadth he demonstrated to me that day also characterized his
scholarship and dealings with others. Despite his bent toward, and
training in, archival work and organization, he looked beyond
individual data to see broad patterns and to develop interpretive
syntheses. His general history of the European Middle Ages, his

study of medieval poverty as a source of heretical movements, and his comparative approach to such major concepts as feudalism all reflect a largeness of mind.

Another quality should be noted here. Manteuffel's integrity as a scholar and as a person was an element of character which even today dominates the memories of those who knew him. It was not simply that he strove for accuracy in his scholarship (though, of course, as a good historian, he did). More than this, he respected his data. He would not allow them to suffer at the expense of a conceptual framework or interpretation. This concern was manifested, on the one hand, in some of the historiographical issues noted below and to which Andrew Gorski refers in his Introduction. On the other hand, it gave rise to some of Manteuffel's most interesting personal observations, especially those expressed in two short statements on the ethics of an historian and on historical responsibility. This integrity as an historian was equaled by his integrity as a person. Though highly successful in the often bruising world of academic and organizational politics, Manteuffel did not achieve this by "using" people or climbing over them on his way up. Instead, he worked with them; he inspired them; he led them; and he left behind only the enemies that a man of character generates among those who cannot equal his qualities.

Let us turn now to historiography and focus upon two specific issues: the question of feudalism and its implications, a problem to which Manteuffel devoted so much attention throughout his career; and the not unrelated question of Manteuffel's position as a responsible historian in "some difficult times" in postwar Poland.

Few terms have been as troublesome in the intellectual and historiographical tradition of Europe as "feudalism." The term itself was developed by lawyers and scholars in the eighteenth and nineteenth centuries as an abstraction, a generalization, to describe a variety of relationships and institutions which had existed, with varying degrees of uniformity and system, in several parts of Europe during the Middle Ages. Derived from the late Latin word *feudum,* which originally referred to the estate in land held by military tenure, the term "feudalism" came to be applied to the personal, proprietary, and governmental elements of the whole of society. It eventually, in some usages, was made synonymous with medieval society as a whole. As one of the "-isms" spawned by the nineteenth century, it came to be a term used variously by various individuals, depending upon what the interests of the user were.

In general, European historiography has divided into three schools of thought about feudalism. One, dominant in German and English scholarship, with some Belgian and American adherents, has focused rather narrowly upon the political, military, and judicial aspects of such institutions as vassalage, the fief, and private jurisdiction. These scholars concentrate, in other words, upon feudalism as a system of decentralized government. A second group, chiefly (though not exclusively) French, has followed the approach of Marc Bloch, the great social and economic historian executed in a Nazi prison camp in 1944. Bloch spoke more of "feudal society" than he did of feudalism, but he understood the latter in terms of a whole society in which economic, religious, cultural, and political elements were centered upon lordship. Feudalism encompassed therefore a broad spectrum of medieval life; it was characterized by "a subject peasantry; widespread use of the [fief] instead of a salary . . . ; the supremacy of a class of specialized warriors; ties of obedience and protection which bind man to man; fragmentation of authority . . . ; and . . . the survival of other forms of association, family, and State." Finally, there is the Marxist tradition. Based in the voluminous writings of Marx and Engels, this approach proceeds from assumptions about the economic determinants of history. In its simplest form, it identifies all postslave and precapitalist society as feudal and uses the term "feudalism" to apply to an economic system which conditions all else: social institutions, politics, religion, and culture. Feudalism is merely a stage in the historical process which will be inexorably, and necessarily, superseded by the next stage. Although the Marxist view, when applied to the Middle Ages, bears some crude similarities to Bloch's views, it is important to note that Bloch made the determinant of feudalism not the economic system (which is more familiarly known as "manorialism" or "seignorialism"), but rather a multiplicity of factors.

Manteuffel was early drawn to the question of feudalism. In 1930 he presented a paper on its late ninth- and early tenth-century Carolingian origins to the national gathering of historians in Warsaw. His approach was legal and political. Much of his early scholarship was similar in character. Then came the catastrophe of the war, in the wake of which Manteuffel, Poland, and the Polish historical profession faced radically changed conditions. The demand was for an economic and social framework in conformity with a political ideology in which the Marxian schema was to be applied to all history.

In these difficult circumstances Manteuffel prospered professionally, rising—as Gorski notes—to become director of the Polish Academy of Sciences' Institute of History. He did so, however, almost in spite of his historical views, for he never acquiesced in the grimly anonymous and rigidly ideological views which were demanded during the late 1940s and early 1950s. He made compromises, to be sure. He could not have survived politically and academically otherwise. In his own approach to the study of feudalism, for example, he adopted a framework which had some affinities with the views of Marc Bloch, but which contained also a sophisticated and refined Marxism. He participated vigorously in the historical debates of this period, defending the integrity of the sources and opposing a simplistic application to them of what is now described by some Polish scholars as "a vulgar Marxism." He demanded that conceptual and ideological frameworks not be applied rigidly and uncritically. Because of the power of his intellect and the political courage he aggressively demonstrated, some of the worst abuses of the official Marxism which characterizes historical writing in other countries in eastern Europe were avoided in Poland. Two examples serve to illustrate this. One is related directly to the question of his work on the nature of feudalism; the other comes within the context of the publication of an "official" *History of Poland*.

Manteuffel's mature thoughts on Polish feudalism were expressed in his article in *Medievalia et Humanistica*, which was published in 1964. There he described feudalism as a kind of social organization in which

the distinctive features . . . would be (1) the predominance of a
natural economy; (2) concentration of the ownership of basic means
of production, which in this case was the land, in the hands of a
privileged class (the great domains); (3) personal dependence of the
peasantry on the landowner, to whom it paid rent earned from the
cultivation of the land, and (4) a low technological level.

While these criteria resemble manorialism more than the feudalism of either of the first two schools noted above, and certainly
conform in a general way to a Marxist definition, Manteuffel's
application of them to the Polish scene was not uncritical. He
refused to see developments in western and eastern Europe as
being identical; he argued that feudalism was not everywhere and
at all times the same thing. He concluded:

> The Polish Middle Ages did not provide conditions in which West-
> ern feudalism could grow, having adopted only Western feudal law
> extraterritorially as it were mainly for the use of aliens resident in
> Poland. Does this indicate that Poland did not have a native feudal-
> ism at all? I think not. . . . We shall try, then, to show that our
> history in later periods created more favorable conditions for the
> development of a native feudalism than in the Middle Ages.

This statement departs sharply from the traditional dogmatic
Marxian assertion that feudalism had necessarily to have been in
evidence in Poland by the end of the tenth century. Manteuffel's
position thus represents an important reformulation of the problem. In other words, he did not try to force the medieval social,
economic, and political development of Poland into a procrustean
ideological bed.

The First Methodological Congress of Polish historians was
held in late December 1951 and early January 1952. Marxist methodological principles were defined and a decision made to publish
a new, multivolume synthesis of Polish history. Eventually Manteuffel was appointed as general editor, with responsibility for the
whole project. Within four years, a trial edition (or *makieta*, in
Polish) was ready. It reflected the restructuring of Polish historiography in conformity with Marxist-Leninist-Stalinist thought.
The hand of politics and ideology rested heavily upon the *makieta*
of the first volume, which extended chronologically to 1764.

Abroad, non-Marxist scholars almost universally condemned it. In Poland, the volume was also subjected to intense debate, both formally, in organized discussions, and informally, in private conversations. When one professor at the Institute of History claimed publically that professional ethics had often been ignored and repeated efforts had been made to falsify history, Aleksander Gieysztor supported him and pleaded for a complete revision of the methods of research and writing.

Manteuffel's position was difficult. As general editor (though he had no direct editorial responsiblity for the first volume), he was ostensibly the sponsor of the project. With a certain vested interest in ensuring its acceptance, he could not appear to be negative about its merits. In fact, however, he had deep reservations. Individuals today suggest he worked privately to ameliorate some of the worst abuses in the volume, but little or nothing of this appears in the public record. The compromises he was able to effect were often ones of degree rather than kind. Whatever his efforts, however, some political changes worked to the advantage of those who favored modifications. The beginnings of de-Stalinization in the Soviet Union and the Polish "thaw" in cultural matters after October 1956 made it possible to weed out some of the most objectionable elements of the *makieta*. When the final version was officially published in 1957 and 1958, it had a more scholarly tenor, appeals to and quotations from the classical *auctores* of Marxism had been drastically reduced, and some of the rigidities of periodization had been softened. Though clearly Marxist in its methodology and organization (volume 1 is subtitled *The Era of Feudalism to the Mid-Eighteenth Century*) and frequently infuriating in its weaknesses, it was nevertheless a major historiographical contribution. That it was as good as it was is in part due to the careful balancing act which Manteuffel was able to perform upon the high-tension wire of Polish academic politics.

Manteuffel's early historical work had a decidedly political and institutional cast. His archival orientation and his early study of the Merovingian and Carolingian monarchies partially explain this approach. But Manteuffel was also very much a product of a prewar historiographical tradition in Poland which was itself dominated by political and constitutional concerns. Thus it is not surprising that when he prepared to write a synthetic history of the origins of early medieval Poland he should do so in that tradition of political narrative. The work he wrote, which Andrew Gorski has now translated as *The Formation of the Polish State: The Period of Ducal Rule, 963–1194,* was closely connected with his teaching in the secret underground university which existed during the Nazi occupation. Although it was only published posthumously in 1976, Manteuffel did not ever intend this to be a "throwaway" exercise; he expected from the beginning that it would be published, probably as part of a larger history of medieval Poland which he projected.

Because it was written some four decades ago and because it stands in what I have suggested is an older tradition, one may be led to conclude that the work is antiquated. It is not. In the first place, it rests firmly upon a thorough knowledge of the written sources, and all of these which are available today were known to Manteuffel. In addition, because his study represents the work of a single, organized mind, it reflects a unified approach and interpretation which fragmented, multiple-author accounts can never match. Finally, it is still a fresh and original historical study because it is not constrained by the preconceived ideological framework which became obligatory after the war. Only in one respect has contemporary scholarship made an advance upon Manteuffel's work. More attention to economic, social, and cultural matters has enriched our understanding of the first two centuries of the Polish state—but without altering or superseding the political narrative Manteuffel provided. It is instructive, for example, to compare his *Formation of the Polish State* with Aleksander Gieysztor's chapters on the same period in the cooperative *History of Poland,* first published in an English edition in Warsaw in 1968. The two historians (the latter the student of the former, both close colleagues through the 1950s and 1960s) complement one another's presentation. One can, therefore, read Manteuffel's work confident that it remains superior in its narration of events and political development to anything else available.

The story which Manteuffel tells in this study is, of course, important for the history of Poland; its significance is also great, however, for the larger question of the formation of Europe. Let us look at each of these in turn. Unlike many of the modern states of western Europe, Poland had no "ancient" history, for its lands and peoples had largely lain outside the sphere of classical civilization. Its history—if by that one understands the written record—begins properly only in the tenth century, with the formation of the state under the rule of the Piast dynasty and its entry into the historical consciousness of Christian Europe. Thus what Manteuffel is writing about is not just a choronological fragment chosen from the larger course of Polish history. He is dealing with the fundamental beginnings by which the future course of the state and nation were shaped. (In contemporary Marxist scholarship, with its emphasis upon "material culture" and with its historical materialism, this distinction between history and prehistory has tended to become blurred. Consequently some of the importance traditionally attached to the tenth century has been deemphasized in an effort to portray this period as part of a larger, longer process.)

For the course of development Manteuffel describes, three elements can be singled out as of particular significance. One was the effort of successive dukes (first Mieszko and after him Bolesław Chrobry) to consolidate their authority. They were originally supported in this by military retainers, who eventually emerged as a new aristocracy or nobility, replacing the older families and tribal leaders. With time, however, that nobility sought greater political and economic power for themselves, inevitably at the expense of ducal power. In the first two centuries of the state, therefore, we see the interplay of centrifugal and centripetal forces within the kingdom of Poland. By the time Manteuffel's narrative ends (and perhaps even earlier, with the death of Bolesław Krzywousty in 1138), the latter had triumphed. Poland was to sink for a century and more into territorial fragmentation, political localism, and regional particularism. Recovery did not come until the late thirteenth and fourteenth centuries; but when it did, it rested in part upon the traditions of Poland as a kingdom and of central power which had been established by the earliest Piasts.

A second element was the goal of establishing the territorial integrity of Poland and defending it against the other emerging states of central and eastern Europe. This is why Mieszko and his successors waged war so constantly. They were driven by a need to establish a territorial unit which comprehended the areas of the proto-Polish tribes, which was of sufficient size to compete effectively with its neighbors, and which was located, with regard to the land and sea trade routes, in a position to be able effectively to exploit the wealth which commercial activity brought. At times the Polish dukes pursued programs of territorial expansion that appear in retrospect to have compromised the territorial integrity of other states in the region. Thus we find Bolesław Chrobry attempting to control Moravia and campaigning in the lands of Kievan Russia. It should be remembered, however, that many territorial distinctions were still very fluid, and also, as Manteuffel so effectively points out, that this policy to the south and east was undertaken with regard to Poland's interests vis-à-vis the Holy Roman Empire. Thus in the period under consideration, Manteuffel explores the origins of some themes of geo-politics which have been deeply influential in the course of Polish history.

A third element, by no means the least important in the long course of the nation's history, was the introduction into Poland of Christianity. Mieszko's conversion probably occurred without deep spiritual motivation. Rather, he recognized the cultural and political importance of the act. Poland gained thereby an international respectability as a civilized nation; it ceased to be an outsider to the emerging Christian civilization of the Latin and Germanic west. Poland therefore became, by culture and religion, an integral part of the western rather than the Byzantine tradition. By contact with more highly developed western centers of culture, education, and art, it was eventually able to assimilate their achievements and produce its own distinctive culture. In addition, the christianization of Poland provided religious sanction for the political framework of strong ducal (later royal) authority in Polish society. The church supported Mieszko's authority as duke, and he and his successors supported its prerogatives within society. By providing organizational models and trained officials, the church helped the duke extend his authority and consolidate his internal administration.

Finally, Mieszko's acceptance of Christianity and the eventual
(though gradual) conversion of his people were carried out in such
a way as to insure religious and even political independence from
any of Poland's neighbors. Poland's direct dependence upon the
Holy See, first as a missionary diocese, later under its own metropolitan, enabled Mieszko and his successors to resist much of the
political dependence which accompanied the extension of the imperial German church, with its proprietary character.

The formation of the Polish state was only one of the things
happening during the period Manteuffel covers. On a grander
scale, out of the crucible of events which followed the collapse of
the Carolingian order, Europe itself was being born. The antique
civilization of Rome had been so culturally and politically debased
in the west in the centuries after Constantine that an ordered
civilization nearly ceased to exist. During the eighth and early
ninth centuries, the ruling dynasty of the Franks tried to create a
new Europe. But the empire of the Carolingians was, in the
telling phrase of Helen Maude Cam, "an anachronism and an
unrealized dream." They failed in their effort. Charlemagne could
not accomplish in a single lifetime all that was needed; those who
followed him were not his equals; and Europe suffered from a
series of renewed invasions. Thus it was not the Carolingian Empire which formed the starting point for the history of medieval
Europe; in many important ways it was the developments of the
following centuries which were the foundation.

Among historians, the tenth century traditionally has had a bad
reputation. James Harvey Robinson, whose textbooks shaped the
historical understanding of several generations of American students, suggested that it was, with one other, "the most ignorant,
the darkest, and the most barbarous period ever seen." It was, in
short, the "darkest of the Dark Ages." But, as Lynn White, Jr.,
remarked in a symposium on the tenth century in 1952, "a lot can
happen in the dark . . . [and] . . . if it was dark, its darkness was
that of the womb." What he was referring to are the facts that in
the generations after 900, new literary, musical, and architectural
forms were developed; new social classes emerged both in the
urban settlements of Europe and in the countryside; religious re-

form was instituted at Cluny and elsewhere which later inspired and transformed Christian society and institutions; commercial activity began to quicken; population started a dramatic rise; verdant buds of intellectual activity sprouted in a number of centers of learning; technological innovation introduced revolutionary techniques to warfare and to farming; and new methods of crop rotation and new crops provided a better-balanced diet. All these things betokened the coming of a new era.

Nowhere else is this sense of promise so evident as in the formation of new states. In the political units that succeeded the Carolingian empire, the political problems of the tenth and eleventh centuries were solved in a variety of ways. In the west Frankish realm, political decentralization gave rise to the feudalization of authority. Feudalism (in a non-Marxist sense) became an element of resistance to the total collapse of the social and political order. While in the short run this phenomenon looks anarchical, it was in the long run to provide the basis for the slow evolution of the French monarchy. In the east Frankish realm, the failure—both dynastic and political—of the Carolingians resulted in the emergence of the German duchies as arbiters of their own fate. It was their leaders, perhaps unwittingly, who helped establish the German monarchy, which, especially under Otto I, successfully dealt with the problems of the Magyar invasions. In the wake of his success, the Holy Roman Empire strove to become the spokesman for and arbiter of the whole of European civilization. On the Italian peninsula, the way in which Carolingian control passed into the hands of the local rulers conditioned the particularism of Italy for centuries to come.

Elsewhere in Europe, the tenth and eleventh centuries saw crucial political developments. The Wessex monarchy in England successfully recovered the shattered remnants of other Anglo-Saxon kingdoms from the Danish invaders. In so doing, the successors of Alfred the Great established a reasonably strong, relatively centralized English monarchy. On the Iberian peninsula, the surviving Christian rulers began the centuries-long work of the Reconquista. On the northern and eastern periphery of the Carolingian world, the consolidation of the Scandinavian states, the creation of a Hungarian kingdom after the Magyar "age of adventures" had come to an end, and the emergence of Bohemia as a stable political unit were all positive developments. The shape of medieval Europe was being defined.

Thus, in tracing the formation of the Polish state Manteuffel was pointing out one important element of what was in fact a civilization in the making. It is worth noting here, as Andrew Gorski does below, that Manteuffel was responsible for what is still the best study of this overall process. The book he edited, *L'Europe aux IXe–XIe siècles. Aux origines des états nationaux,* was the result of a major international conference which he and Aleksander Gieysztor organized in Warsaw and Poznań in September 1965. Papers were presented on all of the major political units in those centuries. Out of that meeting came a picture of Europe as a whole.

It is important to recognize the implication of this last statement. For several generations, scholars have commonly accepted, almost unconsciously, the conclusions of the nineteenth-century German historian Leopold von Ranke. When he thought about what European civilization was, he assumed it was the Latin-Germanic world upon which, he said, "the whole development of our condition down to the most recent times has depended." The implication of the book from the 1965 conference is that what constitutes European civilization is not simply the western European heritage, but also the national and cultural traditions of all the peoples and states whose early formation was discussed in the conference. Thus the present book on the formation of the Polish state is not merely a contribution to Polish history; it is a contribution to European history.

Paul W. Knoll
University of Southern California

Acknowledgments

I wish to express my gratitude to Professor R. V. Burks of Wayne State University for reading the initial draft of my translation and recommending the project to Wayne State University Press; to Professor Stanisław Trawkowski of the Academy of Sciences' Institute of History in Warsaw for his valuable help in the final stages of this translation; to Professor Tadeusz Manteuffel's widow, Maria Manteuffel; to Professor Jerzy Dowiat of the Institute of History; to Mary Van Starrex and the Kosciuszko Foundation for their encouragement and financial support; and to Lucille Jaworowski, who was immensely helpful by offering editorial suggestions and preparing copies of my revisions. My greatest debt is to my wife, Małgorzata, for agreeing, with the cheerful enthusiasm typical of her, to prepare the index.

Introduction

This translation of Tadeusz Manteuffel's "Polska w okresie prawa książęcego, 963–1194" not only attempts to fill a basic gap in the historical literature that is available in English regarding medieval Poland, but also provides a needed Polish perspective. In 1971, the Polish journal *Kwartalnik Historyczny* published a synopsis of a discussion involving a group of eminent Polish historians titled "Obraz Polski w historiografii obcej" [The image of Poland in foreign historiography], pp. 331–53. Aleksander Gieysztor presented an overview in which he lamented the fact that, with few exceptions, Poland has been largely ignored in general medieval studies, or if it has been included, then often only superficially or with distortions. Gieysztor further objected to the tendency among western medievalists to rely on German historiography for a perspective. Admittedly, the linguistic impediment is a major cause for westerners' reliance on non-Polish sources. He also indicated that too often medievalists neglect Polish historiography in forming their perceptions of medieval Poland, accepting instead the interpretations in various west European or even other Slavic historiographies. (Gieysztor certainly had Czech and Russian interpretations in mind.)

It is true that several of Manteuffel's articles and monographs have appeared in French, German, and Italian translations, as have a small but recently increasing number of studies by other Polish medievalists, such as Henryk Łowmiański and Gerard Labuda. Unfortunately, there still are few English translations of Polish historical scholarship or medieval studies that take into regard Polish sources. A notable exception is an original study of the reigns of the last two Piast rulers, Władysław Łokietek and Kazimierz Wielki, by Paul Knoll (*The Rise of the Polish Monarchy: Piast Poland in East Central Europe, 1320–1370* [Chicago: University of Chicago Press, 1972]). Other more extensive presentations of the Polish medieval period available in English are represented by Francis Dvornik's works, particularly *The Making of Central and Eastern Europe,* 2d ed. (Gulf Breeze, Fla.; Academic International Press, 1974); by Stanisław Kętrzyński and Alexander Bruce Boswell's contributions to the medieval section in *The Cambridge History of Poland* (1950); and by the early chapters in the *History of Poland* written by Aleksander Gieysztor, 2d ed. (Warsaw: Polish Scientific Publishers, 1979). These works are either cumbersome and convoluted (Dvornik), too brief and general (Boswell and Kętrzyński), or poorly translated (Gieysztor).

The Manteuffel text should be of interest to both students and scholars of general medieval history. The organization of the early Piast state and the process of West Slav tribal unification and resistance to German territorial expansion during this first period of recorded Polish history are presented. Manteuffel examines Poland against the background of the emergent state system in east central Europe and interprets the consequences of the transitory alliances and frequent conflicts that arose among Bohemia, Hungary, Rus, and Poland, especially in relation to matters of ducal succession and German eastward expansion. Internecine conflicts of dynastic succession in Poland contributed to the dissolution of the unified Piast state. These struggles were further complicated by the challenge of a powerful magnate class to the sovereign rule of the Piasts. The period of fragmentation (1180–1320) persisted until the reconstruction of the Polish state and the restoration of the monarchy under Władysław Łokietek (reg. 1320–1333). Manteuffel begins his narrative with the earliest recorded confrontation along the western Slavic perimeter (963), when Mieszko I annexed various Lekhitic tribes while attempting to restrain German expansion. The narrative ends with the death of Kazimierz Sprawiedliwy (1194) and the legitimation of a fragmented and partitioned Poland, ruled by various branches of the Piast dynasty. Manteuffel also surveys the disruptive political reaction, both domestic and foreign, to the introduction of Christianity and the later establishment of an independent metropolitan in Poland. The general presentation takes the form of a chronological narrative and serves as a substantive introduction to the early Polish medieval period.

Manteuffel abstains from polemics and digressions in regard to controversial interpretations that have especially divided Polish and German historiography, though brief references to such disputations occur in the text. His study is also free of the rigid socioeconomic interpretations which have characterized much of Polish historical scholarship since the end of World War II. It should be pointed out that the monograph was written during the period of the war, but cannot be regarded as outdated. It remained unpublished in Poland until 1976, probably as a consequence of the fact that it was the last extensive work written on the formation of the Polish state before the strictures and conformism of Marxist interpretation were imposed on the postwar Polish academic community. Though the Marxist prescription is no longer so severely uniform, works such as Karol Modzelewski's *Organizacja gospodarcza państwa polskiego, X–XIII* [The economic organization of the Polish state, tenth through the thirteenth centuries] (Wrocław: Ossolineum, 1975) preserve the formula. Manteuffel bridled against such obligatory obeisance.

In the biographical notes to *The Crucible of Europe* (Berkeley: University of California Press, 1976), Geoffrey Barraclough made a brief comparative comment on a collection of essays published in Warsaw, though in a French edition, under the title *L'Europe aux IXe–XIe siècles. Aux origines des états nationaux* (Warsaw, 1968). Among works dealing specifically with the ninth and tenth centuries, this book—to which Manteuffel contributed an article and of which he was the editor—is, according to Barraclough, "outstanding [and] . . . particularly valuable for the emphasis it places on political and social developments in eastern and south-eastern Europe." Manteuffel elaborated and developed his article in the section "Polska wśród nowych państw Europy" [Poland among the new states of Europe] in the volume *Polska Pierwszych Piastów* [Early Piast Poland], 3d ed. (Warsaw: Wiedza Powszechna, 1974). The most recent publication of a work by Manteuffel was his contribution to the medieval section of *Zarys historii Polski* [An outline of Polish history] (Warsaw: Państwowy Instytut Wydawniczy, 1979), edited by Janusz Tazbir. The earlier monograph that I have chosen to translate is broader in scope, considerably more detailed, and not at variance with his later contributions.

The polonized branch of the Manteuffel family originated in the nobility of Livonia, an area that was annexed to the Polish-Lithuanian commonwealth in the sixteenth century. Tadeusz Szoege-Manteuffel was born in the city of Resekne (Polish Rzeżyca; German Rositten), Latvia on 5 March 1902. He was tutored at home and later attended gymansia in Petrograd and Warsaw. In 1919 Manteuffel enrolled at the already repolonized University of Warsaw, but in July 1920 he volunteered for military service in the Polish-Soviet war. As the result of a wound, Manteuffel's right arm was amputated. He returned to the University of Warsaw the following year to continue his studies and pursued his interest in medieval studies by participating in seminars on the Merovingian period conducted by Marceli Handelsman (1882–1945). Manteuffel also had begun to work as an assistant in the Archiwum Oświecenia in 1921 and eventually became its director before it was destroyed by German aerial bombardment in 1939. This was the first of several archives with which Manteuffel was associated during his academic career.

His first articles appeared in 1924 and 1925 on topics pertaining to the French chronicles and stressed the interpretation of primary sources through strict linguistic analysis. Manteuffel's doctoral dissertation on the unification policies of Clotaire II was also published at this time. He spent the academic years 1924–25 and 1925–26 conducting medieval research in France, Italy, and England. From September 1926, Manteuffel conducted proseminars in European medieval history at the University of Warsaw, in which Aleksander Gieysztor eventually became a participant. In 1929–30, Manteuffel traveled to Paris and Heidelberg to conduct further research. Between 1924 and 1939, he published forty-one articles and monographs on medieval and archival topics. Among those of special interest are the articles which analyze the historical paradigm of feudalism in its western and eastern European variants and offer specific definitions of their diachronic political, social, and economic characteristics.

In his unfinished memoirs, Manteuffel describes the first German attacks on Warsaw in 1939, and in one especially poignant passage he tells how, after the archives were destroyed by German bombardment, the salvageble books and manuscripts were carried like human bodies on stretchers to the shelter of a yet undamaged library. Virtually all of these materials were later lost during the Warsaw Uprising of 1944. After the war, Manteuffel was closely associated with efforts to rebuild these collections. During the German occupation Manteuffel became a member of the Związek Walki Zbrojnej (Union of Armed Struggle), later known as the Armia Krajowa (Home Army). He was the secretary and a contributor to the underground publication *Wiadomości Polskie* [The Polish news] of the Bureau of Information and Propaganda (BIP-AK). Toward the end of 1940, Manteuffel's mentor, Marceli Handelsman, asked him to organize a history curriculum and teach in the Polish underground university. Manteuffel agreed, beginning with a group of only six students. The numbers increased between 1940 and 1944 to ninety students, and the number of participating faculty rose from three to twelve. Stanisław Kętrzyński, another well-known archivist and medievalist, was among them.

In his memoirs, Manteuffel also describes several incidents which occurred toward the close of the war as Soviet troops were advancing toward Poland. He was led to believe that he had been marked for assassination by a Falangist group, Narodowe Siły Zbrojne (National Armed Forces), because of his leftist views. It is highly questionable whether the Armia Krajowa then retained any control over this splinter group. Manteuffel fled Warsaw and went into hiding in July 1944; he did not return until six months later, after the Warsaw Uprising, to a house which, to paraphrase his own words, had been reduced to dust and emptiness and inhabited by mice and sparrows.

On 1 September 1945, Manteuffel held his first class in more than six years at the University of Warsaw. In February of the same year he had begun the task of reestablishing the Institute of History in devastated Warsaw. As its director from 1945 to 1955, Manteuffel faced overwhelming difficulties in recruiting a professorial faculty—only two of the original eight professors of history at the University of Warsaw remained in Poland after the war. The remaining six either perished or emigrated; among the emigrés was Oskar Halecki. The university facilities and library collections had been almost completely destroyed.

During the severest period of Stalinization, Manteuffel chaired the Humanities Department (1948–50) and was prorector of the University of Warsaw (1951–53). He was elected to the newly created Polish Academy of Sciences and later joined its presiding body. In 1953 Manteuffel restructured the Institute of History and was able to secure its independence from the University of Warsaw. During the decade following the end of World War II, Manteuffel engaged in a series of confrontations with dogmatic Marxists from governmental ministries and within the academic community who rejected any variance from the ideological and methodological tenets of Marxist historical materialism. At various academic congresses in 1951 and 1952, sharp attacks were leveled at the historical methodology of the interwar period and at members of the history faculty who represented the "old guard." Manteuffel rose to the defense of his deceased mentor, Marceli Handelsman, and argued persuasively against a uniform and mandatory formula for historical interpretation. This period of stress certainly contributed to the first heart attack which Manteuffel suffered in 1955. He resigned from the directorship of the Institute of History but continued to teach at the University of Warsaw until 1968. In addition to his editorial work, Manteuffel produced nearly sixty more articles and monographs after 1955. His *Średniowiecze powszechne. Do schyłku XV wieku. Próba syntezy.* [The middle ages to the end of the fifteenth century: An attempt at a synthesis] (Warsaw: Polskie Wydawnictwo Naukowe, 1958) was published after the political thaw in eastern Europe and represented one of the first works to appear in postwar Poland that was a compromise between an orthodox Marxist interpretation and the methodology which was organic to earlier Polish historical scholarship.

Manteuffel had a significant role in Polish intellectual life through his administrative and organizational functions at the University of Warsaw and various other institutes and academic societies. In steadfast adherence to his principles, he jeopardized his professional life by opposing the preconceived Marxist formulas that became axiomatic in Polish academic scholarship. Some historians chose to protest silently by confining themselves to annotating primary sources, which was officially regarded as an innocuous exercise. But in a series of confrontations, the intensity of which contributed to a serious illness, Manteuffel argued that a historian's ethical norms could not be supplanted by political formulas arrived at on the basis of contemporary events. Manteuffel eventually was compelled to compromise his position and make pragmatic concessions, at least in appearance, but if scholarship was supposed to be entirely obsequious to a political ideology, then Manteuffel's work certainly was not exemplary of this tendency. Perhaps it is somewhat difficult to reconcile Manteuffel's insistence on unconstrained academic integrity and ethical norms with the fact that he maintained an official status generally reserved for individuals with more conformist views. In any case, his role in the Polish academic community of the late 1940s and early 1950s is complex. He was determined to rebuild postwar Polish historiography without acquiescing to the difficult political circumstances of the period. He was a principled and determined individual with a strong sense of mission, and his life is a vivid and distinguishing thread in the fabric of Poland in the twentieth century.

In the last fifteen years of his life, Manteuffel directed his research away from feudalism and toward ecclesiastical organization and heretical sects. His study of the Cistercians in *Narodziny herezji* (Warsaw: Polskie Wydawnictwo Naukowe, 1963) has been translated into German, French, and Italian.

Tadeusz Manteuffel died on 22 September 1970.

Note on the
Translation

It was my intention to convey as closely as possible the content and form of Manteuffel's text, but I have taken some minor liberties with it. Polish rhetorical devices which do not translate well into English, particularly repetitions, have been omitted; some sequences of short paragraphs in the original have been combined in the translation. Some other alterations also seemed appropriate, such as a change in the title, which I have expanded from the more literal "Poland during the Period of Ducal Rule, 963-1194." In several places I have omitted dense—or, at the other extreme, merely glancing—word descriptions of geographical data. The long passages have been replaced by maps which present the same information visually. The monetary term "mark" replaces the Polish *grzywna* (which had a value of approximately 190 grams of silver). Where they seemed appropriate, dates have been added. I have also provided a brief introduction facing the first page of the translation itself. These are the only changes from the Manteuffel text. The headings of the various sections and their order have been preserved.

The idiosyncratic web of transliteration practices and inconsistent equivalents for Slavic proper and place names is disturbing and has no simple remedy. I see no advantage in adopting a latinized form like Boleslas for the Polish Bolesław or Czech Boleslav, or in reducing three Slavic forms, such as Świętopełk (Polish), Svatopluk (Czech), and Sviatopolk (Russian), to one, especially when using the original contributes to textual clarity. Occasionally reference is made to individuals with cognate names (for example, Bolesław-Boleslav) in the same paragraph or section of the text, which may create an ambiguity. For the sake of maintaining distinctions, therefore, I have preserved the original forms of Polish, Czech, and Hungarian names unless there is a commonly used English form, which then takes precedence (for example, Stephen I of Hungary rather than István I). Russian names have been transliterated according to the Library of Congress method with the exception of iotized *a,* which is given as *ia,* except in initial position, where it is *ja.* The Polish epithets for the Piast princes are given in the original form, with a bracketed English equivalent on first reference. The names of foreign-born Polish princesses appear in the Polish form.

Place names present similar problems. Manteuffel uses only Polish forms throughout his text. I have used the Polish names for the cities located along the Baltic littoral and in proximity to the Oder River and its tributaries, with the German equivalent bracketed on first reference. Whenever there is a familiar or anglicized form, such as Oder for Odra, Vistula for Wisła, Upper Lusatia for Milsko, it is preferred. In the section pertaining to the struggle for succession in Volynia and Galicia, I have used Galicia to refer to the principality with the city of Halicz at its core. Tribal names have also been anglicized. The appendixes to the translation provide further clarification and reference.

It is somewhat disappointing that Manteuffel did not provide a bibliography. However, the undocumented references which appear in the body of the text are clarified in Appendix D. Inasmuch as the translation is intended for an English-speaking audience which lacks a working knowledge of Polish, I beg to be excused from providing a bibliography of additional Polish sources. The bibliographic information provided in Appendix D lists translated titles of the original works. An informative aid to works on Polish history available in English is Norman Davies, *Poland, Past and Present: A Select Bibliography of Works in English* (Newtonville, Mass.: Oriental Research Partners, 1977). I must mention, however, the two Polish primary sources cited in the text: the chronicles of Gall Anonim (d. ca. 1116) and Wincenty Kadłubek (d. 1223). A translation of only the first five chapters of Gall Anonim's chronicle by Francis D. Lazenby appeared in the *Polish Review* 11, no. 4 (1966):5–9; I am not aware of any published English translation of Kadłubek's work. The translations of passages from both chronicles in the present text are my own.

the formation of the polish state

[Charlemagne had subjugated the Saxons and Bavarians and crushed the Avars at the eastern limits of his vast empire by the year 804. The Carolingian Empire at that time extended from the Atlantic Ocean to the river Elbe, beyond which were the Slavs. This empire rapidly began to dissolve and by the year 843 was divided into three parts among Charlemagne's successors. The eastern area became the patrimony of Charlemagne's grandson, Louis the German (840–876). After contesting for hegemony over parts of Italy and the "Middle Kingdom," which lay between West and East Frankland, a German kingdom ("Regnum Teutonicorum") arose in 911 with the election of the non-Carolingian Conrad of Franconia (911–918). A new empire was being created in East Frankland principally from the duchies of Saxony, Bavaria, Swabia, Franconia and Lotharingia. During the process of consolidating the German duchies, Henry I of Saxony (918–936), who was also king of Germany, dealt the invading Magyars their first serious defeat, forced Bohemia into submission, and began the *Drang nach Osten* against the Polabian Slavs and Lusatian Sorbs. The Magyars earlier had menaced the German duchies and had already crushed the first Slavic state of Great Moravia by 906. Henry's son, Otto I (936–973) forcefully extended the German sphere of influence and was crowned emperor in 963. It is in this context that Manteuffel begins his narrative.]

1

The Western Slavs

In this period we encounter the Western Slavs embroiled in an intense conflict with their western neighbors.

The reign of Charlemagne undoubtedly represents a critical juncture in the course of German expansionism, inasmuch as Charlemagne absorbed the Saxons and Bavarians into the Frankish empire and decisively prevented German expansion to the west, directing it instead toward the east.

From the time of the Avar dispersion [A.D. 796], the entire eastern border area of the Carolingian Empire was controlled by the Slavs, who also had penetrated deep into Frankish territory and colonized large tracts of land along the upper Main. The Slavs had not yet developed a culture equal to their western neighbors nor established a political state, but remained in a fragmented, tribal arrangement which facilitated Charlemagne's defense of the eastern boundary of his vast empire. In order to secure the extensive frontier area between the Alps and the Baltic Sea, Charlemagne established the Danish and Avarian marks where the empire was most vulnerable. The two marks were connected by a fortified line of frontier outposts know as the *limes sorabicus*. [See map 1.]

The military fortifications along the eastern boundary of the Carolingian Empire initially were intended to function as defense posts. Their purpose was to maintain a stable frontier, which Charlemagne was able to achieve along its entire length. The *limes sorabicus* was also an ethnic boundary; the Slavs who had settled to the west of this line were quickly germanized. The marks soon expanded from their original defensive role. From the time they were annexed to the empire, they also functioned as the furthest extended bulwark of a German offensive. The Avarian mark or Ostmark was the first to assume this new role when its margraves turned their attention toward the possible annexation of the Slavic lands along the Danube. The first independent Slavic state had been established there, the State of Great Moravia—which is the precise name under which it first appears in history. Mojmír founded this state in approximately A.D. 830. His successors, Rastislav and Svatopluk, significantly extended the boundaries of the state by annexing Pannonia and Bohemia to the territories in Moravia and Slovakia already settled by the Slavs. At the height of its expansion, the State of Great Moravia also included the lands of the Lusatian Sorbs and the Lekhitic Silesians and Vistulans. [See map 2.]

This large Slavic state was rather short-lived. Though it had been forced to defend itself against German incursions from the moment of its inception, it fell in A.D. 906 when it was attacked from the east by a new enemy, the Magyars. These lands were then either in part occupied by the Magyars or paid tribute to them.

The Magyar invasion, which cut off the Western Slavs from the Southern Slavs, also prevented the Bavarians from expanding along the Danube and forced them to remain only defensively disposed in the area for quite some time.

The situation along the northern *limes sorabicus,* where the Slavs had not been immediately threatened by their western neighbors, was quite different. There the Slavs were the belligerent element. During the ninth century they had invaded Saxony many times. News of the destruction of Hamburg in A.D. 842 by the Slavs and Normans spread throughout the West. After the fall of Great Moravia, the Magyars ruled over a significant part of this state and launched a series of incursions into the Carolingian provinces, while the Slavs from the areas of the Elbe and Saale became allies of the Magyars. This was an especially arduous period for German efforts at unification, and these incursions coincided with the collapse of these efforts. Saxony became dominant among the principalities which were striving for independence. Under the reign of the Liudolfing family, which since 919 had combined the hereditary rights of the prince of Saxony with the elected crown

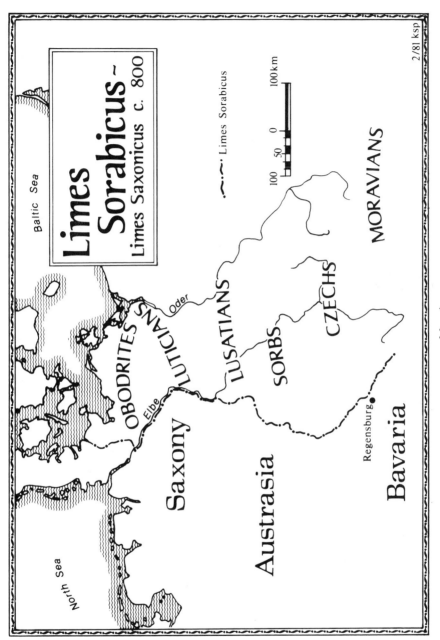

Limes Sorabicus ~
Limes Saxonicus c. 800

Baltic Sea

North Sea

OBODRITES

LUTICIANS

Oder

Elbe

Saxony

LUSATIANS

SORBS

CZECHS

MORAVIANS

Austrasia

Bavaria

Regensburg●

`··~·` Limes Sorabicus

100   50   0   100 km

Map 1

of the German kingdom, Saxony coalesced internally and became a formidable external force. By the year 933 the Saxons had succeeded in eliminating any further threat of a Magyar incursion, but the Germans in the south remained vulnerable to this threat up to the middle of the tenth century. In preparing for a decisive confrontation with the Magyars, Henry I tested his troops in battle against those Slavs who had allied themselves with the Magyars.

These Slavs belonged to two distinct ethnic and linguistic groups, the Sorbo-Lusatian and the Lekhitic. The tribes which composed the Sorbo-Lusatian group lived in the territory between the Saale in the west, the Erzgebirge and Sudeten mountains in the south, the Kwisa [Queiss], Bóbr [Bober], and Odra [Oder] rivers in the east, and the Spree in the north. The Lekhitic group was composed of two separate subgroups, Polish and Polabian. The Polabians were the only group which neighbored on Saxony, and were composed of the Obodrites, who inhabited a wedge of land between the lower Elbe and the Baltic Sea, and the Luticians (Veletians), settled to the north of the Lusatian Sorbs and to the east of the Obodrites in the territory between the Elbe and the lower Oder. [See map 3.]

The Lusatian Sorbs first fell victim to German attacks. They were splintered into many separate tribes and succumbed individually to the superior German force. In order to maintain control over the defeated tribes, Henry I established burgwards where he garrisoned large numbers of pardoned brigands and other criminals. They were free to abuse and coerce the Slavic population in any way, so long as they defended the territory which had been annexed by the Germans.

In 928 Henry attacked the Luticians. Compared with the Lusatian Sorbs, they represented a more homogenous front, since all the tribes in the area cooperated in a coalition. Unfortunately, several tribes inhabiting the area adjacent to the Lusatian Sorbs broke from the alliance during this time. Without the aid of these tribes, the Luticians fell to the Germans after a stubborn defense.

After subjugating the Lusatian Sorbs, Henry stood at the boundary of the Czechs. After the collapse of Great Moravia, the Czechs

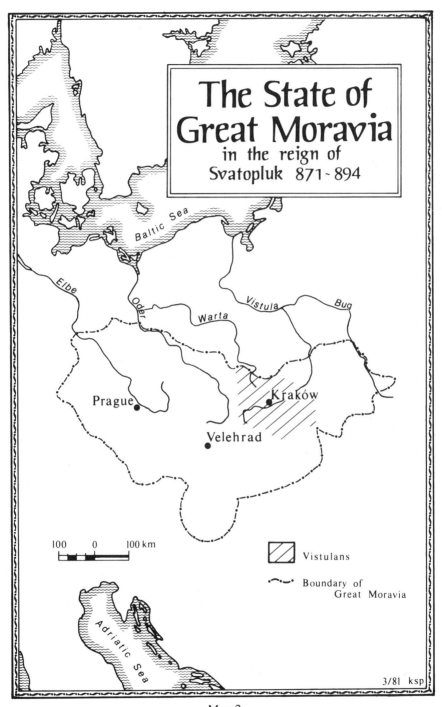

The State of Great Moravia

in the reign of Svatopluk 871-894

Baltic Sea

Elbe

Oder

Warta

Vistula

Bug

Prague

Kraków

Velehrad

100   0   100 km

Adriatic Sea

Vistulans

Boundary of Great Moravia

3/81 ksp

Map 2

had been largely united by the ducal family of Prague, the Přemyslids. However, Henry would not tolerate the existence of an independent Slavic state bordering on territories which had recently been conquered. Such a state could easily become the ally of any resistance to assimilation. Henry entered into an agreement with the prince of Bavaria, invaded Bohemia in 929, and laid siege to Prague. The attack was so sudden and unexpected that the Czech prince, Václav, surrendered without resistance and became a German vassal. He agreed to pay an annual tribute and acknowledged the supremacy of the bishop of Regensburg over the Christians in his lands. Boleslav I accepted the same terms in 935 when he succeeded his brother, Václav, who had been assassinated.

The Slavs in the northwest refused to submit to German subjugation. They rebelled several times and, during the Magyar invasion of Saxony in 933, they were able to free themselves temporarily from German rule. This was a temporary success, because the victory over the Magyars permitted the Saxons to regain these lost territories within a short time.

Henry's conquests led to the complete subjugation of only the Lusatian Sorbs; the remaining members of the West Slavic group were compelled to pay an annual tribute.

Henry's death while he was conducting a campaign against the Polabian Slavs became a rallying cry in a general revolt which was supported by the Czechs. This rebellion was bloodily suppressed by Henry's son and successor, Otto I. In order to prevent a similar outbreak in the future, he proceeded to colonize the conquered areas. He placed the church under German control and divided the territory into two marks, with Herman Billung and Gero as their rulers. Herman Billung was given the northern territory adjacent to the Obodrites and Luticians, whereas Gero received the southern area inhabited by the Lusatian Sorbs, who had just recently been conquered. Both margraves were belligerent toward the Slavs and were not at all reluctant to employ treachery and deceit. Gero was especially expert in these tactics.

The German relationship to tributary or vassal tribes was somewhat different. According to Tadeusz Wojciechowski's splendid characterization, it was based on the following six objectives: 1) maintain the custom of dividing the state among all the sons of a vassal prince in order to prevent a single large territory from forming; 2) actively support all claims to dynastic succession in order to have a reason to intervene and permit the German king to act as arbitrator between pretenders; 3) increase tribute by auctioning the throne to the pretenders who sought German aid; 4) exacerbate the rivalries between the various Slavic groups; 5) interfere in the creation of a monarchy and unified state in any of these lands; and 6) prevent the rise of an independent church organization which could serve as one of the greatest supports for establishing an independent state. This policy was designed to protect the Germans from the rise of an adversary that could prevent their expansion to the east. It likewise laid the foundation for the eventual and complete annexation of these vassal and tributary states to the empire.

While the Polabians were contending with eastward German expansion, the Poles, who were separated from any non-Slavic adversary by a belt of dense wilderness and marshes and by areas settled by other Slavic peoples, were undergoing a process of internal consolidation. They were composed of the following tribes: the Polanie, Silesians, Vistulans, Łęczycans, Kujavians, Mazovians, and to some extent, the Pomeranians. The Pomeranians, however, represented a link between the Polabians and the Poles, since there were characteristics which the Pomeranians shared with one group as well as the other. [See map 3.]

The Polanie inhabited the lowland areas of the Warta [Warthe]; the Silesians lived along the river Silesia by Sobótka Mountain; and there were related smaller tribes, known as the Dziadoszans, Bobrzans, Opolans, and Lubuszans, which occupied a wide area around the settlements of the Silesians. The Vistulans controlled the upper and middle parts of the Vistula with a city of the same name at the center; the Kujavians settled the shores of Lake Gopło, bordering on the south with the Łęczycans. (Both of these small tribes can be considered offshoots of the Polanie.) The Mazovians occupied the lands along the middle and lower Vistula, predominantly on the eastern shore. Finally, the Pomeranians occupied the Baltic shore between the mouths of the Oder and Vistula.

Geographical factors contributed to a particularism which persisted for a very long time among these Polish tribes. Their existence was internalized, centering on a unifying religious cult and originally was governed by the *wiec*, a convocation of all free tribesmen, and later, when security demanded a greater consolidation of power, they were governed by an elected prince.

The tribe consisted of clans (*ród*)—that is, a group of individuals who were related by blood and descended from a common ancestor. The *starosta* (or *starszyna*) stood at the head of the *ród*. He had both judicial and military power over the clan, but exercised this power most frequently in conjunction with an assembly of elders. There was a highly developed sense of solidarity within the clan. There was no concept of private ownership of land; therefore the clan was a common propiretor and engaged in a communal economy. Members of the clan were obliged to defend any other member from injustice. The custom of blood vengeance against murderers was slowly disappearing; it was being replaced by payment of ransom (*główszczyzna*) to be divided among the members of the clan. In areas where the religious cult was especially strong, where trials were conducted, or where the clans gathered in case of danger, a stronghold called a *gród* was built. The territory which was inhabited by a single clan was called the *opole*.

An organized state emerged relatively late among the Polish tribes, as it did similarly among the other Slavs. The theory of a foreign invasion, which supposedly brought about the rise of the Polish state, has been definitively rejected by scholars; however, there is no question that one of the causes for the formation of an organized state from among the Polish tribes was an external threat. This threat on the one hand, and the internal dynamics within the more populous tribes on the other, resulted in the assimilation of the weaker tribes.

The earliest nucleus of this kind was the Vistulan tribe. Unfortunately, our knowledge concerning it is very limited and in large part depends on rather unreliable legends—about the founder of Kraków (Krak), or the prince of the Vistulans (Wisław), and so on. But apart from the legends, there are accounts from several sources describing Saints Cyril and Methodius's mission to

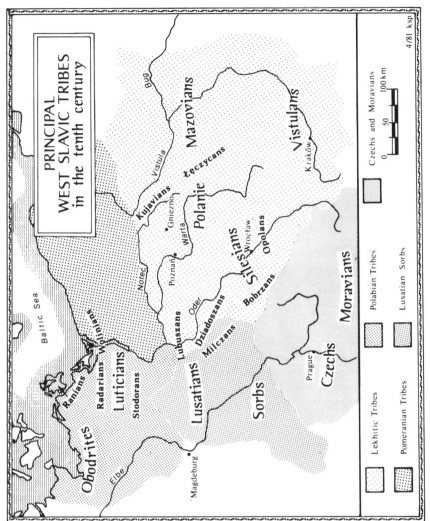

PRINCIPAL
WEST SLAVIC TRIBES
in the tenth century

Baltic Sea

Obodrites
Ranians
Radarians
Luticians
Stodorans
Wolinians
Elbe
Magdeburg
Lusatians
Sorbs
Lubuszans
Milczans
Dziadoszans
Oder
Bobrzans
Silesians
Opolans
Wrocław
Prague
Czechs
Moravians
Kraków
Vistulans
Vistula
Łęczycans
Polanie
Warta
Poznań
Gniezno
Kujavians
Noteć
Bug
Mazovians

Lekhitic Tribes

Pomeranian Tribes

Polabian Tribes

Lusatian Sorbs

Czechs and Moravians

0   50   100 km

4/81 ksp

Map 3

Moravia. These sources provide an account of an unnamed powerful Vistulan prince, who opposed the efforts of these missionaries and only accepted Christianity after he was taken prisoner by the Moravian prince, Svatopluk. This tale permits us to conclude that in the second half of the ninth century there existed an independent Vistulan state, that the Vistulans were defeated by the Moravians, and this, in turn, resulted in the spread of Christianity in the area. The borders of the Vistulan state and its later fate are unknown, and any attempts to piece together its history have not gone beyond conjecture.

The Polanie certainly began to make their presence known at approximately the same time as the Vistulans. But again, there is a paucity of historical records; instead, the legends about Popiel, Piast, and others have been preserved. These legends, which were familiar to the earliest Polish chronicler, Gall Anonim, induced him to present the genealogy of the princely family in such a way as to link the first recorded Polish ruler, Mieszko, with the legendary Piast, the founder of the dynasty. In this genealogy Mieszko is the fourth successor in a direct line from Piast; therefore, we can hypothesize that the events which led to Piast's assuming power among the Polanie occurred some time about the middle of the ninth century. It could also be assumed that Piast took power in a state which had already been organized by Popiel and his predecessors.

Tadeusz Wojciechowski presented a hypothesis concerning the unusual name "Piast," concluding that it was not really a name, but rather the title of a high-ranking member of the prince's court, known in Latin sources under the terms *nutritor,* or *paedagogus.* Therefore, the *piast,* whose role corresponded to that of the Frankish *major domus* or even the Russian *kormilets,* fulfilled that function during the Popiel dynasty, just as the Carolingian *major domus* did during the Merovingian dynasty. Seizing an opportunity, the *piast* deposed Popiel and executed his family.

The new dynasty's contribution was the annexation of the more distant Polish tribes by the Polanie.

2

Initial Contact with the West

In Widukind's *History of the Saxons* [*Res gestae Saxonicae*], we find the following entry for the year 963: "Wichman was eagerly received by them [the Radarians] and defeated the more distantly settled pagans in many battles. Twice he defeated King Mieszko who ruled the Slavs called Licikawiki.* He killed his brother and took enormous tribute." This is the first mention of Poland in the sources of the period.

The events of 963, which raised the curtain that had obscured Poland from full view, proved Mieszko to be one of the three most powerful rulers among the Western Slavs, together with Boleslav I of the Czechs and Nakon of the Obodrites. His state included Wielkopolska and the Lubusz [Lebus] territory, Eastern Pomerania, the Sieradz and Łęczyca territories, Mazovia, the Sandomierz territory, and the Grody Czerwieńskie. The lands which were ethnically Polish, but outside these boundaries, were Silesia and the Kraków and Przemyśl territories, which were then under Czech control, and Western Pomerania, which fiercely defended its tribal independence. Poland was separated from areas of German expansion by the lands of the Luticians and Czech Silesia, from the Prussians and Jadzwings by swamps and dense wilderness, and from the Russians by lands which had not yet been claimed by any state. Poland, therefore, had the time to fortify and organize itself internally in peace. This process, as can be

---

*This name is variously interpreted in our historiography. The predominant view before the Second World War was presented by J. Widajewicz: it referred to one of the Pomeranian tribes which was subordinated by Mieszko and inhabited the area of the confluence of the Oder and Warta rivers.

47

concluded on the basis of several premises, had been going on for at least two generations.

The center which provided the stimulus to unite the Polish territories was Wielkopolska, which was relatively densely populated. As early as the beginning of the tenth century, the Polanie had brought under their control the neighboring tribes of Kujavians, Mazovians, Vistulans, and Pomeranians. The state which the Polanie established took its name from them—Polska.

The force preserving the unity of these somewhat varied tribal groups was in the person of the prince, who was descended from the Piast dynasty of the Polanians. The part of German historiography which strives to diminish Polish achievements injects the theory of the role of Norman invaders. However, this theory cannot be substantiated, since historical and prehistorical data resulting from research such as that concerning the anthroponymy of the Piasts indicate that the hypothesis is entirely unfounded; rather, there is proof beyond doubt of the Slavic origin of the Polanian dynasty.

Widukind's brief reference does not explain the reasons for the conflict between Mieszko and the Radarians, who were led by Wichman. Only an analysis of the situation along the northeastern boundary of the empire at that time illuminates these events and allows us to understand them. This border area was rife with frequent skirmishes between the Germans and the Slavs, and the quarrelsome Saxons even fought among themselves. It was rather predictable that these conditions would create an ideal opportunity for adventurers, who eagerly left their own homelands to seek their fortunes in less confining circumstances.

Wichman was precisely such an individual. At odds with his uncle, Herman Billung, because of an inheritance claim, he next became an implacable enemy of Otto I, who had supported Billung. Wichman first joined the cause of Otto's German opponents, but when they were defeated, he refused to submit and fled to a foreign court. He conspired against Otto in France and then looked for support among the pagan Obodrites. He was declared an enemy of the state, but he was returned to favor through Gero's intercession. Wichman was also related to Gero, who offered him asylum. This did not inhibit Wichman from further collusion with Otto's enemies. In these circumstances, Gero could no longer harbor his impossible relative, and he induced him to join the Luticians, hoping to protect Otto from some further escapade of Wichman and to ensure certain advantages for himself.

Wichman joined the Radarians, which was a Lutician tribe that had already often caused serious problems for the Germans. Gero had planned to subject the remaining independent Lusatian tribes in 963 and needed to reduce the threat of intervention by the Radarians. He recognized the need to turn their attention elsewhere. Through Wichman he drew the Radarians into a confrontation with Mieszko, who at this time was attempting to bring Western Pomerania under his control and was already competing for control of the mouth of the Oder. Mieszko's campaign was a serious threat to the independence of the neighboring Lutician tribes.

Gero's plans ended in complete success. Wichman led the Radarians in two incursions into the territory already under Mieszko's control and twice defeated his army. Mieszko's brother was killed during one of these battles, and the victorious Radarians took enormous spoils. Meanwhile Gero exploited the Radarian commitment against Mieszko and defeated the remaining Lusatian tribes.

The relationship between Wichman and Gero was no secret to Mieszko. He had to protect himself from any further disastrous consequences which could result from the defeats of 963 and to find an ally who would not only support him in his campaign against the Luticians, but who could also protect him from the Saxons' machinations. Mieszko decided to seek a rapprochement with the emperor, which was also in Otto's interest, because his involvement in Italy demanded peace in the east at any price. Gero assumed the role of intermediary and became the emperor's representative in the negotiations. He concluded a formal Polish-German alliance directed against the Luticians. The agreement (in Zygmunt Wojciechowski's opinion) contained a clause whereby the emperor renounced all intentions to expand any further into Western Pomerania so as not to jeopardize Mieszko's strategic position. In return, Mieszko agreed to pay an annual tribute from the territory which was then defined as the land "which stretched to the Warta."

The anti-Lutician alliance forced Mieszko to assess his relations with the Czechs, who were allies of the Luticians. It is possible that the agreement between Mieszko and the Bohemian prince, Boleslav I, which was later reinforced by marriage between Mieszko and Boleslav's daughter, Dubrawka, in 965, was mediated by the Germans. This was due both to a weakening annexationist policy following Gero's death on 20 May 965 and the division of his mark into five parts. The empire was compelled to rely on a strengthened Polish ally.

The alliance did not actually deprive Poland of its sovereignty, but it brought Poland into the political orbit of the empire, establishing it as a mark sui generis. Mieszko understood that in this situation a pagan Poland would be in an especially disadvantageous position. In order to prevent his already dependent position from worsening, he decided to be baptized as a Christian. Perhaps his recent bride, Dubrawka, influenced his decision.

The Christianization of Poland (966) proceeded according to the prince's wishes and was not opposed in the country. On the contrary, the rapid progress of the missionary effort seems to indicate that there was already a substantial Christian community that supported the work which proceeded under the auspices of the prince's court. Mieszko entrusted proselytizing to the Czech clergy. However, there is no doubt that a significant majority of the missionaries was recruited from the German clergy of the Regensburg diocese, because it would have been an almost impossible task for the recently converted Czechs to conduct a missionary effort on so large a scale by themselves. Jordan, perhaps a native of Flanders, was appointed missionary bishop of Poland and directed the arriving clergy. His tasks were to convert the country to Christianity and establish a church administration. According to his title, Jordan was not subject to any German metropolitan, but was directly responsible to the Apostolic See.

The alliance of 963 was further strengthened by later agreements with the Czechs that gave Poland certain political advantages. Mieszko finally was able to gain temporary control of

Western Pomerania with the aid of Czech reinforcements. However, Mieszko was not able to annex this territory to Poland because of the Pomeranians' fierce sense of independence, and he could only impose his sovereignty on them for the time being. The Luticians under Wichman's command again tried to contain Polish expansion, but they were defeated in 967 and Wichman was killed while in retreat.

Mieszko endeavored to maintain good relations with his German neighbors, and the Saxon chronicler Thietmar mentions his deferential relationship with Gero's successor, the margrave Hodo. The increasing power of the Polish prince must have been a serious source of concern for the margrave, because in 972 he crossed the Oder and attacked Mieszko. Hodo met unexpectedly strong resistance, and he barely escaped with his life after his army was defeated at the battle of Cedynia [Zehden].

The Polish victory had a profound impact on the German principalities and caused the emperor, who was then in Italy, to intervene. He was concerned about preserving the integrity of the eastern frontier boundaries and demanded that the antagonists refrain from further combat and appear at an inquiry in Quedlinburg.

The inquiry took place in the spring of 973 and revealed the emperor's partiality. He not only absolved Hodo but demanded that Mieszko deliver his son, Bolesław, to the imperial court as a guarantee of Mieszko's loyalty. Mieszko was offended by the emperor's decision, but he was most concerned about his son's welfare. This concern would be the only possible explanation for why Mieszko sent an envoy to Rome, who conveyed a lock of Bolesław's hair to the pope. Mieszko intended to place his son symbolically under the protection of the Apostolic See. When Otto I died several months later, Mieszko and his Czech brother-in-law, Boleslav II, declared their support for Henry the Quarrelsome, the prince of Bavaria, who aspired to the now vacant imperial throne. Furthermore, Mieszko broke the agreement that he had signed in 963 with Otto and refused to continue paying tribute for Western Pomerania.

Henry the Quarrelsome's position was apparently quite weak. The first attempted revolt against Otto II was quickly suppressed, and Henry, as the leader of the rebellion, was deprived of his hereditary rights and imprisoned in one of the imperial castles. However, Otto had much more difficulty with Bohemia and Poland. Several retaliatory campaigns against the Czechs ended in failure until the emperor finally reached a compromise with Prince Boleslav in 978.

Meanwhile, Dubrawka had died in 977 and consequently relations between Poland and Bohemia had weakened. The compromise of 978 did not involve Mieszko and gave the emperor a free hand eventually to punish his rebellious tributary. Otto II took advantage of Mieszko's isolation and organized the first German military campaign against Poland in 979. However, he met strong resistance and was forced to withdraw. Mieszko's success was all the greater because he was acting completely alone, without the aid of his earlier Czech ally.

Otto II's attention was focused on the Apennine Peninsula and that preserved Poland's success, since the emperor depended on a peaceful eastern boundary. Otto abrogated his claim and sued for peace. The peace was consolidated by Mieszko's marriage to Oda, the daughter of the margrave Dietrich of the Nordmark. Dietrich's antipathy toward Boleslav II of Bohemia and the marriage of his daughter to Mieszko would indicate a clear decline of Polish-Czech relations. This soon led to a military confrontation, which resulted, as Karol Buczek suggested, in the annexation of the Karków and Przemyśl territories by Poland. The newly acquired territories were placed under the administration of Mieszko's oldest son, Bolesław.

This set of circumstances on Mieszko's southern boundary would explain events which have not been satisfactorily clarified in Polish historiography regarding the Russian invasion in 981 that resulted in the loss of the Przemyśl territory and the Grody Czerwieńskie. As Stanisław Zakrzewski correctly observed, Prince Vladimir of Kiev was married to a Czech princess and, in an alliance with the Přemyslids, could have undertaken a campaign against Mieszko with the aim of displacing him from this newly acquired territory. In undertaking this action Vladimir was perhaps equally concerned about establishing a new route to Constantin-

ople through Hungary, which would substitute for the Dnieper
route that was now blocked by the Pechenegs.

Otto's death in 983 led to a brief reconciliation between Mieszko and Boleslav II, since both continued to be supporters of
Henry the Quarrelsome, a perennial candidate for the German
crown.

Meanwhile, Mieszko also arranged a marriage between his son
Bolesław and the daughter of Rigdag, the margrave of Meissen,
in order both to enhance his position among the Saxon nobility
and to establish a future dynastic claim on Meissen.

Relations between Henry the Quarrelsome's supporters soon
became discordant. When Boleslav II took advantage of his position among Henry's supporters and took control of Meissen in
984, Mieszko's plans were frustrated, and he crossed over to the
imperial camp.

There were other reasons why Mieszko sought an accommo-
dation with the emperor's widow, who now acted as regent for
her young son. The Polabian revolt of 983 brought about the
collapse of German power between the lower Oder and Elbe
within just months and became a formidable threat to the Polish
state, especially to the recently conquered territories of Western
Pomerania. Mieszko made every attempt at reconciliation with
the empress and in 985 reinforced German troops in their campaign against the Luticians.

In succeeding years—986 and 987—Polish troops aided the empire in its struggle with Bohemia for control of Meissen and were
a potent force in regaining this territory for the designated successor to the mark, Eckhard.

Meanwhile, a new enemy was threatening Mieszko along the
lower Oder. The Danes had taken Wolin [Wollin] at the mouth of
the Oder in 985 and had established a colony called Jomsburg.
Mieszko voluntarily decided to honor the agreements of 963 and
traveled to Quedlinburg in 986 to submit to the authority of the
emperor and offer gifts of tribute. Though circumstances were
somewhat different, the situation of 963 essentially repeated itself.
Mieszko previously had not been satisfied with only a German
alliance to contend with the Luticians, but had attempted to secure

Bohemian aid. Now, in order to impede the Danish invasion, he endeavored to bring the Swedes into a coalition. In order further to consolidate the alliance, Mieszko gave his daughter in marriage to the Swedish ruler, Eric the Victorious.

Additional facts in the primary sources are rather clouded regarding the Polish-Danish conflict. It still can be inferred, however, that Mieszko was able to defend himself against the Danish threat and not only captured Szczecin [Stettin], but also took Jomsburg.

Relations with the Czechs had been tense since the Meissen affair and led to another military confrontation in 989. Both sides went into battle with foreign allies in their ranks: the Czechs were supported by the pagan Luticians, while the Poles were allied with the Germans and perhaps a Czech dynastic family from Libice which challenged the Přemyslids. The war continued to 990 and ended in a Polish victory. Mieszko not only defeated the Czechs, but he also forced them to retreat from Silesia, the only ethnographically Polish area which still remained under Czech control. It is quite possible that Mieszko's son Bolesław also conducted a campaign at the same time along the southern boundary, and when Mieszko had taken Silesia, Bolesław had also brought Slovakia under his control.

The newly acquired territory had to be consolidated quickly. Made wiser by the experience of 972 to 973, Mieszko decided to seek support outside the empire. He turned to the Apostolic See, with which he previously had established closer ties. After his successful campaign against the Czechs, Mieszko placed all of Poland under the protection of Rome, with the hope that the papal curia would successfully aid in preserving its totality. Perhaps Mieszko also linked a request for an independent church province for Poland and recognition of Poland as a kingdom to his "donation." However, these are suppositions which are not supportable by source material. Mieszko's act of donation to the Apostolic See has not been preserved. The document is extant only in a brief abstract in which the names of both persons and places have been distorted. Mieszko's name is strangely deformed to "Dagome," which has been the source of vacuous ideas and hypotheses regarding the genealogy of the Piasts.

Mieszko was present at the emperor's court in Quedlinburg in 991 and later joined Otto III's retinue in his campaign against Brandenburg. These are the last known activities of the aging prince, who died on 25 May 992.

Mieszko was overshadowed by the brilliant figure of his son and successor. No matter to what extent the reign of Bolesław Chrobry [the Brave] is associated with the flourishing young state, nevertheless it must not be forgotten that the foundation of this powerful structure was laid by Mieszko. He had finally united all the Polish lands. He brought Poland into the Roman family of civilization, and he was able to resist powerful German pressure from its very beginnings and preserve the suzerainty of his young state. He is justly acknowledged as the architect of the Polish state.

3

Emancipation from
the Empire

Poland fell into a state of anarchy after the death of its founder. Divisive forces broke out that had been contained up to this point by the strong hand of the prince. Not only did Mieszko's direct heirs struggle for supremacy, but they were also challenged by tribal princes who previously had been displaced by the dynasty. Mieszko's entire life's work might have been nullified and a resurgence of earlier tribal divisions threatened Poland. The danger was all the more acute since neighboring states began to meddle in these internal conflicts.

Bolesław Chrobry, Mieszko's son from his marriage to Dubrawka, brought this menacing situation under control. He had the advantage of age over his half-brothers and half-sisters from his father's marriage to Oda. While they were still children, the twenty-five-year-old Bolesław was a mature man. Even during his father's lifetime he had been trusted to rule an independent province and had gained experience in both military and diplomatic matters under his father's tutelage. His three marriages and two divorces, which clearly were pursued for political ends, offer some proof that he used his acquired skills to full advantage when he assumed the task of unifying the state against the opposition of his stepmother and her sons, as well as against other pretenders. It was not an easy task and it obviously was not to be completed quickly.

Bolesław's first concern was to prevent the emperor's possible intervention on behalf of Oda and to restrict any aid which Oda might obtain from her German relatives. Immediately after his father's death, Bolesław sent reinforcements to the emperor for his campaign against Brandenburg in 992, while he also attempted to prevent the heirs of the margrave Dietrich from succeeding to power in the Nordmark. He was able to achieve both ends and avoided German intervention. But these were not the only threats. Though little is known about the circumstances, Oda maintained close relations with Vladimir of Rus. The danger of an attack on the eastern boundary did not permit Bolesław to participate personally in the emperor's campaign against Brandenburg, but instead he moved east with the larger part of his army. It is not known whether this was a demonstration of saber-rattling or whether there was in fact a military confrontation.

Prince Boleslav II of Bohemia had taken a rather unclear position in regard to the events in Poland. His early benevolent attitude toward his nephew later underwent a radical change. Perhaps he was influenced to some extent by the strong sympathy for Bolesław Chrobry displayed by the princes of Libice who were the Přemyslids' rivals in Bohemia.

In any case, for one reason or another, Boleslav II declared his opposition to Bolesław Chrobry, which may have resulted in the temporary seizure of Kraków by the Czechs.

Despite all of these diverse complications, Bolesław was able to gain control of the situation. Oda and her children were expelled, and two Polish magnates, Przybywój and Odylen, who had aided her were blinded for rebellious and treasonous acts.

Pomerania resisted Bolesław's power the longest, but eventually it too succumbed. All the lands which had constituted his father's state in time came under Bolesław's control. [See map 4.]

Bolesław must have conducted an internal pacification of the state before 995 (perhaps in 994), because he participated in a campaign against the Obodrites when Otto III required him to send reinforcements. Similar summons were sent to the Přemyslids of Prague and the Slavníkovci of Libice. The elder Slavníkovec, Soběslav, personally participated in the campaign against the Obodrites, but Boleslav II only sent reinforcements under the command of his son. His pretext for remaining in Prague was old age; however, the truth of the matter lies elsewhere. Boleslav II was a reluctant ally in the campaign against the Polabians, with whom he had maintained good relations over a long period of time. His true intention was to take advantage of Soběslav's absence from Bohemia in order to come to a final confrontation with the independent principality of Libice. Ignoring the emperor's universal truce for the duration of the Obodrite campaign, Boleslav attacked Libice and brought it under his control. The Vršovci, a family devoted to Boleslav, at his instigation murdered all the members of the Slavníkovci that had been taken prisoner.

News of this tragedy reached Soběslav while he was still engaged in the Obodrite campaign. It was impossible for him to return to Bohemia, and Soběslav proceeded to Poland with his retinue and surviving kin. Bolesław Chrobry welcomed him hospitably and established his family in Poland. According to tradition, Soběslav became the founder of the noble family of Paluk.

The fall of the Slavníkovci brought another member of the family, Wojciech [Vojtěch (Cz), Adalbert (E)], the bishop of Prague, into a closer union with Poland. Wojciech felt uncomfortable in his elevated position in the church hierarchy and had previously attempted to resign from his bishopric and devote himself to a monastic life. On this particular occasion, however, he was compelled to return to his episcopal duties, but he was not to remain in Prague for long. When another conflict arose in his diocese, he again left Prague for Rome in 995. It was in Rome that Wojciech met the young emperor, Otto III, upon whom his unworldly nature made an enormous impression. Otto's own association with monks and ascetics was a search for relief from the emptiness of earthly existence. The understanding between them quickly grew into a deep friendship. But even the emperor could not protect Wojciech from the church hierarchy's demands, which required the bishop to return to the diocese he had abandoned. However, because the extinction of his family in Libice made it impossible for Wojciech to return to a state ruled by the Přemyslids, the Apostolic See gave its approval for him to undertake a mission to a pagan land. Wojciech chose Poland as the country from which he would conduct his work, the country which had become a second homeland to those of his relatives who had escaped assassination. Perhaps Bolesław Chrobry also had influenced his decision, which could be inferred

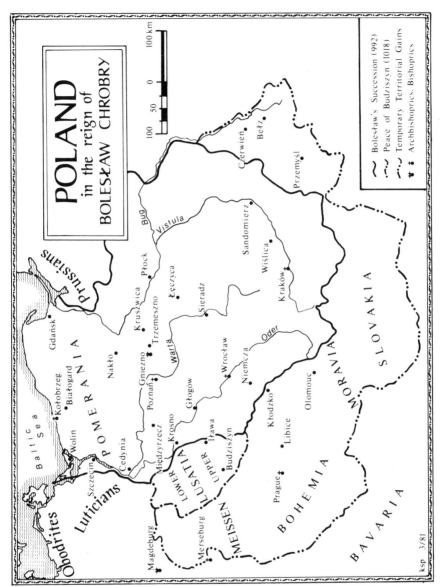

POLAND
in the reign of
BOLESŁAW CHROBRY

100 km
100   50   0

Bolesław's Succession (992)
Peace of Budziszyn (1018)
Temporary Territorial Gains
Archbishoprics. Bishoprics

Prussians

Baltic Sea

Obodrites
Luticians

Gdańsk
Kołobrzeg
Białogard
Wolin
Szczecin
Cedynia
Międzyrzecz
Krosno

POMERANIA

Nakło
Kruszwica
Gniezno
Poznań
Głogów

LOWER
LUSATIA
UPPER

Iława
Budziszyn

Magdeburg
Merseburg
MEISSEN
Kłodzko
Libice
Prague

BOHEMIA

Olomouc

MORAVIA

BAVARIA

SLOVAKIA

Płock
Trzemeszno
Łęczyca
Sieradz
Warta

Wrocław
Niemcza
Oder

Kraków
Wiślica
Sandomierz

Vistula
Bug

Czerwień
Bełz
Przemyśl

Map 4

ksp 3/81

from the various hagiographies of Wojciech that suggest a warm relationship had existed between them for a long time. Bolesław depended on drawing the bishop of Prague to Poland in order to reinforce the process of Christianization and to act as the patron of missionary activity in lands that were the object of Polish expansionism.

Wojciech devoted his several months' stay in Poland to evangelical work and founded the Benedictine abbey in Trzemeszno [Tremessen]. He first considered undertaking his missionary work among the Luticians. However, this area was in the German domain of proselytization and in the spring of 997 he left for the land of the Prussians. He traveled by ship from Gdańsk to the Prussian coast, and shortly after landing, he was attacked by the fanatically pagan Prussians and died a martyr on 23 April. Two men who accompanied Wojciech managed to escape and returned to relate what had occurred. Chrobry then ransomed Wojciech's body for its weight in gold, and it was entombed in the church of the Holy Virgin Mary in Gniezno.

Because of his reputation in western Europe, Wojciech's martyrdom turned the Christian world's attention to Poland. His death deeply affected the emperor, who at the time was near the eastern boundary of the empire, preparing a new campagn against the Luticians. Otto's first thought was to honor the martyr by funding the construction of a monastery in Aachen which was to bear Wojciech's name. After his return to Rome, he requested that the church consider the possibility of Wojciech's canonization. Bolesław doubtless threw his support behind this initiative and took advantage of the prevalent atmosphere to send his emissaries to Rome in order to request that a new church metropolitan be established, with its center where Wojciech's body was interred. The metropolitan was to embrace all the lands under Bolesław's control and consolidate the rule of the Piasts over the newly acquired territories.

The moment for this kind of action was well chosen, and what Mieszko had not been able to accomplish was realized during Bolesław's reign. At one of the next synods in Rome, the decision was made to establish a new metropolitan, and most probably without any major change in Bolesław's plan of divisions into dioceses.

Wojciech's brother, Gaudenty, was soon after consecrated a bishop. This must have occurred before December 999, because in documents pertaining to the abbey at Farfa, signed on 2 December 999, one of the signatories was Archbishop Gaudenty of Saint Wojciech's Cathedral.

To honor the memory of his now canonized friend, Otto undertook a pilgrimage to his tomb early in the year 1000 and on the same occasion participated in the act of erection of the new metropolitan. Fourteen years after the event, the Saxon chronicler Thietmar wrote an account of the emperor's journey.

> Once past the boundary of the Milczans, he [the emperor] came to the land of the Dziadoszans, where Bolesław came to greet him with boundless cordiality and prepared quarters for the emperor in a place called Iława. The manner in which the emperor was regaled by him and then escorted through this land to Gniezno is something impossible to believe or to describe. When he saw the city from a distance, he walked piously in bare feet and was received with extraordinary honors by bishop Unger [the Polish missionary bishop, Jordan's successor], and when he was led into the church he begged, pouring forth tears, for Christ's mercy through the intercession of the holy martyr.

Gaudenty's installation was to take place in Gniezno and be followed by the installation of the bishops of the newly created dioceses: Poppon of Kraków, Jan of Wrocław [Breslau (G), Vratislav (Cz)], and Reinbern of Kołobrzeg [Kolberg]. Unger protested the limitation of his powers and was not made subordinate to the new archbishop. The boundary of his diocese was strictly delineated and was to remain in existence only through Unger's lifetime. The substance of the imperial and papal privileges that defined the position of the newly organized church were announced to the assembly at Gniezno. Otto renounced his authority as emperor over the church in Poland, which included the power of lay investiture and the right of determining church organization in conquered pagan territory.

The secular aspect of the emperor's visit to Gniezno was no less important. Otto III, who interpreted the mission of the empire in entirely different terms than his predecessors, openly broke with an annexationist policy in the east. He was determined not only to respect the sovereignty of neighboring states, but to include them in a great federation, which was to have as its primary goal the propagation of the Christian faith. The emperor obviously would remain sovereign in this federation. But Otto designated a key role for Poland and relieved Bolesław of his obligation to pay an annual tribute. He placed a diadem on Bolesław's head and put in his hands a nail from the Holy Cross and Saint Mauritius's lance. Otto recognized Bolesław as a full-fledged member of this newly conceived empire.

This act should not be equated with a coronation elevating Bolesław to a king. It simply did not have that meaning, which is obvious from Chrobry's efforts after the emperor's departure to obtain a crown for himself from Rome. However, this in no way minimizes the political significance of these events, which the Saxons understood very well. They were opposed to Otto III's concept of such an empire, and their opposition was conveyed in Thietmar's severe criticism of the emperor's actions.

> Oh, how sad it is to compare our ancestors with ourselves. During the lifetime of our extraordinary Hodo, his [Chrobry's] father, Mieszko, never dared to enter a house in a coat, in which he thought [Hodo] may be present and he never dared to sit when Hodo stood. Only God could forgive the emperor [Otto III] that he made his tributary [Bolesław Chrobry] a lord and elevated him to a degree that he forgot the basis of his father's relations, gradually daring to put in bondage those who were his betters and baiting them with the vanity of money, taking their freedom and making them slaves.

The emperor's stay in Gniezno gave Bolesław occasion to display his wealth and generosity to his foreign guests. Gall Anonim, author of the oldest Polish chronicle, described Chrobry's generosity.

> Having finally come to the end of the banquet, he ordered his servants to gather all the gold and silver wares—namely cups, goblets, bowls, horns—from the tables of the three-day feast, for there were none of wood, and offered them to the emperor to honor him, not as a princely gift. And he also ordered his servants to

collect those drapes, tablecloths, rugs, carpets, napkins, towels, and all that had been used at the table settings and to take them to the emperor's rooms. And he also presented him with many other wares of gold and silver of various designs and robes of many colors, ornaments never before seen, and precious stones, and he offered so much of all of these things that the emperor considered these boundless gifts a miracle. And he presented such splendid gifts to his princes that he made these friends into closer friends. But who could count the amount or the kind of gifts he gave to these lords when even not one of their very numerous servants went away without a gift?

Gall Anonim's description doubtlessly was exaggerated in the legends which grew for over a hundred years. In any case the emperor's reception must have been genuinely splendid, since even contemporary German chroniclers agree in their references about its unprecedented grandeur. After approximately a week's stay, Bolesław escorted the emperor to Magdeburg, which the retinue reached on 25 March, Palm Sunday, 1000.

In order further to improve upon the successes he achieved during the Congress of Gniezno, Chrobry endeavored to obtain a crown from Rome. The legation, with the abbot Astryk-Anastazy as principal legate, was sent at the end of the year 1000 or the beginning of 1001, but it did not succeed. Because of Astryk's intrigues and betrayal (which are not known in detail), the crown that was intended for Poland was bestowed on Hungary, whose ruler, Stephen, had similarly petitioned Rome for a crown. This was a very heavy blow to Bolesław's ambitious plans, and the significance of this political defeat was magnified by Stephen's marriage to Giesel, Henry of Bavaria's sister. Henry was the leader of the German opposition hostile to Otto III's eastern policies. All of these things pointed to the increasing influence of the camp which opposed the emancipation of the Polish state and put Bolesław's plans in doubt. But the real catastrophe came with the premature death of the emperor on 23 January 1002, which closed the chapter on the plans of this young dreamer. It is not surprising that Chrobry was deeply grieved over his death, recognizing the change of direction in Polish-German relations.

4

The Pursuit of a Crown

Otto III's death released all the forces that had opposed his concept of the empire. In Italy, only several weeks after the emperor's death, Arduin of Ivrea made a challenge for the imperial crown. In Germany the situation was complicated by the fact that, besides Henry of Bavaria, the only possible successor in Otto's line, there were two more contenders: Herman, the duke of Swabia, and Eckhard, the margrave of Meissen. Eckhard's candidacy seemed the most substantial because he could rely not only on the support of the Saxon nobility with his brother-in-law Bernard at their head, but also on the benevolent attitude of the deceased emperor's closest family, represented by his brother-in-law Ezzo, the palatine of Lower Lotharingia.

Henry of Bavaria attempted to rally support for his cause and, cognizant of the assistance which Mieszko had provided his father, he turned to Bolesław Chrobry, promising to give him Meissen as a tributary state in return for his aid. This was a proposition which conformed with Bolesław's political aspirations at the time.

The situation was suddenly altered because of Henry's strongest opponent's death. Eckhard was murdered on 30 April 1002. Perhaps this assassination of a dangerous rival was provoked by Henry himself. Eckhard's death permitted Henry to concentrate all his forces against Herman of Swabia, and he quickly forced him to concede.

Bolesław Chrobry was fully aware that changes in German policy would occur with Henry's accession to power, and he decided to safeguard his western boundary by taking control of the broad area to the west of the Lusatian Gate. Bolesław exploited the civil war in the empire and the conflict which arose among the assassinated Eckhard's heirs in order to occupy Upper Lusatia and Meissen in 1002. Bolesław attached so much importance to these territories that he was willing to control Meissen and Upper Lusatia as German fiefs. With this proposal in mind, Bolesław traveled to a diet of the Saxon nobility in Merseburg at the end of July. Henry by then had no intention of honoring his previous promise, and he agreed to allow Bolesław to retain control only of Upper and Lower Lusatia. He granted Meissen to Eckhard's brother, Guncelin, a friend of Bolesław. Henry dealt with Eckhard's sons perfunctorily by conceding the district of Strzała [Strehla] in Meissen to Eckhard's oldest son, Herman, and agreeing to his marriage to Chrobry's daughter Regelinda, whereby the Strzała area would be granted to Herman as part of Regelinda's dowry.

Behind the facade of this compromise, a treacherous plan was set in motion, and assassins waited in ambush as Bolesław was returning from Merseburg. Only through the aid of some Saxon allies was he able to escape with his life. Seeing Henry's hand in this, Bolesław retaliated by burning the city of Strzała in Meissen and taking the population into captivity. The political situation at the time did not permit Henry to react to these events.

The confrontation came a year later, when the more immediate cause was Bolesław's policy toward Bohemia. Because of the tense relationship with Germany, Bolesław realized it was mandatory to protect Upper Lusatia and Silesia from attack from two possible directions: from Germany and from Bohemia. In order to achieve that end there was only one course of action—to turn Bohemia into a Polish mark on its southwestern flank. This could be achieved either by military occupation or by subordinating the Bohemian princes politically. If Bolesław could establish himself south of the Sudeten mountains, it would provide him with a base to attack Meissen from the south.

Bolesław's cousin, Boleslav (III) the Red, ruled Bohemia at that time. While Eckhard, the margrave of Meissen, was still alive he had often intervened in the internal affairs of Bohemia, and Boleslav the Red could always rely on his support. After his death Bohemia became fertile ground for violent internal conflicts. Boleslav the Red could no longer control the situation and virtually became a puppet in the hands of the magnates, who imposed their will on him. The conflict intensified to the point that, toward the end of 1002, Boleslav was forced into exile, and the magnates elevated Vladivoj in his place. Vladivoj had earlier fled to Poland for political reasons. On his return it became apparent that the new prince was mentally and physically debilitated, and he soon died. Inasmuch as Boleslav the Red's half-brothers were not able to establish themselves on the throne because they lacked German support, the magnates turned to Chrobry with a request to intercede in negotiations with the exiled prince. An agreement was reached and Boleslav's ducal powers were restored. He did not refrain from avenging himself upon his political enemies, and in the beginning of 1003 he attempted to eliminate the Vršovci family, which had opposed him. Those who escaped execution appealed to Chrobry for help. Bolesław again agreed to intervene, but he realized that he would not be able to bring the Czechs into a closer union with Poland by relying on the Přemyslids. He decided to remove them from power and occupy the entire country militarily. Under the pretext that Boleslav the Red planned a military campaign against Poland, Chrobry ordered him to be blinded and then journeyed to Prague, where he was proclaimed prince by the magnates.

Chrobry now controlled both Bohemia and Moravia. Slovakia had been under his control since 990. Bolesław's territorial gains created a buffer mark, which defended the corridors of invasion of actual Polish territory.

The considerable growth of Chrobry's power disturbed Henry. Because he was personally conducting the war against Arduin, for the time being he sent only an emissary to Bohemia, instructing him to demand that the Czechs take the oath of a vassal state. In the event they should decline, he was to threaten them with war. Chrobry refused to submit and obviously demonstrated that he intended to emancipate himself from all German control.

Since Bolesław's relationship to the empire was such that war was imminent, he decided to exploit the disputes within the factionalized German-Roman empire. Because there were so many factions among both the Germans and the Italians, Chrobry could depend on allies within the empire itself. Among these were the margrave of Nordgau, Henry of Schweinfurt, his cousin, Ernst, and the emperor's own brother, Bruno. Bolesław could also rely on the support of the margrave of Meissen, Guncelin. Henry, on the other hand, prepared his great offensive against Bolesław by forming an alliance with the pagan Luticians.

Henry began his military campaign in August 1003 with an attack on Bolesław's German allies. Despite the Polish reinforcements he received, Henry of Schweinfurt was defeated and fled, first to Bohemia and later to Hungary. Bolesław attacked Meissen, thinking that he could occupy it with little resistance. He was misled, because Guncelin refused to surrender his capital to the Poles, which forced Bolesław to withdraw. Henry organized a retaliatory campaign against Upper Lusatia in January 1004, but because of heavy snows he halted the campaign after ravaging the border area.

The necessity of undertaking a campaign in Italy postponed another Polish-German confrontation for several months. After his immediate success south of the Alps, Henry returned to Germany by June 1004 and decided to conduct a general campaign against Poland, beginning in August. According to the plan, the Bavarians were to strike directly at Bohemia, while the remainder of the army was to gather at Merseburg and then move against Lower Lusatia under Henry's own command. It soon became evident that this plan was a cover for the true strategy, because, at the last moment, instead of marching on Lusatia, Henry attacked the poorly fortified border area of the Bohemian Forest and penetrated deep into the country. The pretender to the Bohemian throne, Jaromír, the oldest brother of the blinded Boleslav the Red, was a member of Henry's retinue. At the news of the return of a Přemyslid, the Czechs took up arms and attacked the unsuspecting Poles, killing the garrisoned troops that Bolesław had stationed in the major cities. This action forced Bolesław to abandon Prague, which was then taken by the Germans without a struggle. On 8 September 1004, Jaromír took the oath of a vassal from Henry and in return received Bohemia as a fief.

After this success, Henry moved against Upper Lusatia with Czech reinforcements and laid seige to its main city, Budziszyn [Bautzen]. The garrison capitulated, after a short and heroic defense, with the condition that it be allowed to return to Poland unhindered. All of Lusatia was in German hands. Despite the fact that this campaign had denied Bolesław his latest territorial gains and forced him back to Poland's ethnic boundaries, Henry had no intention of stopping at this point. He intended to destroy Bolesław's power completely, and he announced a new campaign against Poland for the following year.

The point of assembly was Leitzkau, near Magdeburg. By mid-August 1005, the German armies had moved eastward and were joined by Czech and Lutician reinforcements along the way. Bolesław waited near Krosno [Crossen], where he took a defensive position at a fording point on the Oder. When the Germans discovered an undefended position at a place where they were able to ford the river, Bolesław had to abandon his camp and retreat quickly in a northerly direction. Henry followed in close pursuit, through Międzyrzecz [Meseritz] in the direction of Poznań. Bolesław avoided a direct open-field confrontation but constantly harrassed the Germans by attacking their supply trains, and Henry was finally compelled to request a truce. The conditions of this agreement are unknown, but the results were hardly what the Germans expected in any case. The proof lies in Thietmar's statement that Henry "concluded an unfavorable truce and returned with his saddened army, bringing with them the dead." We can conclude that the Germans had to remain content with Bohemia and Upper and Lower Lusatia, which they had occupied the preceding year, while Bolesław was able to maintain his hold over Moravia.

The loss of Slovakia to the Hungarians is definitely connected to this Polish-German conflict. It is impossible to determine precisely when it occurred. Since Slovakia was still in Polish hands in 1001 and by 1007 was under Hungarian control, the obvious conclusion is that its loss resulted in some way from the Polish-German war at that time. It is unknown whether Slovakia was lost during a successful Hungarian invasion or whether it may have been the price which Bolesław paid to preserve Hungarian neutrality.

The peace agreement was short-lived. Henry provoked the breach in 1007 under the pretext that he felt compelled to aid the Czechs and Luticians, who were being threatened by Bolesław. Henry also aided the Wolinians, who had rebelled against Bolesław. He exploited these circumstances in April by demanding changes in the conditions of the peace agreement, and when Bolesław rejected his demands, Henry abrogated the peace.

Bolesław did not hesitate to take immediate action against the Germans. In May he invaded the area near Magdeburg and returned with large numbers of prisoners. Bolesław was now convinced that these German garrisons were quite weak. He intensified his attack and soon after reoccupied Upper and Lower Lusatia.

Henry was not able to counter Bolesław's invasion because he had to contend with a revolt that had broken out simultaneously in Lotharingia, which forced him to remain in the west for almost a year. He was not able to return to Saxony until 1009, and then he also had to arbitrate disputes among the nobility before he could prepare for a campaign against Poland. These disputes brought about far-reaching changes in the marks. Guncelin, the margrave of Meissen, was accused by his nephews of having entered into some kind of an agreement with Bolesław, and he was deposed and imprisoned. The Nordmark was given to Bernard, the brother of Mieszko's widow, Oda.

The significance of these changes was obvious to Bolesław, and he launched a surprise attack against Meissen immediately after Guncelin was imprisoned. Bolesław's attack was not successful, and Meissen was soon after given to Guncelin's nephew, Herman. Despite the fact that he was Bolesław's son-in-law, Herman was Henry's faithful supporter and contributed to entrenching the German position in the east.

The war with Poland was not a unanimously popular issue. There were especially strong reservations concerning the use of the pagan Luticians in the campaign. A letter written by Saint Bruno of Querfurt to Henry II presents evidence of this opposition. Bruno, who was born and raised in the eastern border area and devoted his life to missionary work among the pagan neighbors of Poland, voiced his indignation over this alliance between a Christian monarch and a pagan people against Christian Poland:

> Allow me to say without loss of your imperial favor, how can you reconcile persecuting a Christian [Bolesław Chrobry] and maintaining a friendship with a pagan people [Luticians]? What kind of agreement can there be between Christ and Belial? What likeness is there between light and darkness? How can the satanic Swarożyc join with the commander of the saints—yours and our Saint Mauritius? How can the holy lance be carried next to satanic banners drenched in human blood? O king, do you not consider it a sin that Christian heads—it is shameful even to speak these words—should bow before satanic banners? Would it not be better to seek the fidelity of such a man [Bolesław Chrobry], through whose aid and counsel you could receive tribute from this pagan people and lead them toward sanctity and Christianity?

Henry viewed Bolesław's power as too great a threat to German interests in the east to give any consideration to idealists such as Saint Bruno. The next campaign against Poland was planned for the summer of 1010, and at its conclusion proved to be one of the least successful. Only the Czechs under Jaromír joined the German cause. The Luticians refused to send aid because their relations with the Germans were worsening at the time. Even more important was the withdrawal of support for the campaign by several bishops; even Henry, who was exhausted by an illness, was unable to participate. The campaign became a feeble expedition limited to ravaging a wide area of open terrain west of the Oder, and its only success was regaining a part of Lower Lusatia lost in 1007.

The antagonists spent the ensuing months preparing for the next campaign and rallying allies. In an attempt to counter the Germans' Hungarian ally, Chrobry concluded an agreement with Vladimir of Rus in 1007, perhaps through Saint Bruno's benevolent mediation. The agreement was consolidated by the marriage of Vladimir's oldest son, Sviatopolk, to one of Bolesław's daughters.

Further complications arose for Henry in 1012. At the instigation of the magnates, Jaromír was exiled on 13 April by his brother, Oldřich, who had returned from Poland. Despite this unfavorable sequence of events, a new German campaign was launched against Poland in July 1012. The situation portended failure; the Germans had lost both of their previous allies, the Czechs and Luticians, and Henry was again forced to return to the west, where a new revolt had broken out in Lotharingia. The Saxon nobility hesitated in beginning their offensive and lost the initiative. Bolesław took advantage of the flooding Elbe, which cut off the marks from aid from the west, and attacked the recently refortified city of Lubusz. Bolesław stormed and looted the city and then retreated to Poland with his prisoners. When Henry returned to Merseburg in the fall, it was already too late to undertake a retaliatory campaign. He had first to resolve the conflict between Jaromír and Oldřich, and when he was certain that the new Czech prince intended to take the oath of vassalage and faithfully fulfill his obligations, Henry ordered Jaromír imprisoned and placed in the custody of the bishop of Utrecht. Bolesław's only advantage from the change of rule in Bohemia was the Czechs' temporary neutrality in the 1012 campaign.

Events in Rus also absorbed Bolesław's attention. The mood at Vladimir's court was shifting against Poland, and Sviatopolk and his wife were imprisoned, accused of political machinations aimed at Vladimir. In February 1013, Bolesław sent a legation to Magdeburg to request a truce when he realized that Henry would soon be required to leave for Italy to be crowned as emperor. Bolesław sent his son Mieszko, designated as his successor to the throne, as head of the legation. Henry agreed to allow Bolesław to retain the territories he had taken in conquest, but only under the condition that they become German fiefs. The emissaries further agreed upon the date when Bolesław was to appear at the emperor's court to take the oath of a vassal and determined who the German hostages would be to guarantee Bolesław's safety while he was in Germany.

The ceremony took place in Merseburg on the first day of Pentecost. At its conclusion Bolesław carried a sword before Henry in the procession to the church, fulfilling the honorary function of swordbearer.

Several other matters were discussed at the meeting in Merseburg. Bolesław promised to provide Henry with reinforcements for his Roman campaign, and in exchange he received a promise of aid for his planned campaign against Rus. Perhaps Bolesław's relationship to the Apostolic See was also discussed; it would have pertained specifically to carrying out the objectives of the Congress of Gniezno (1000). The agreements were consolidated in accordance with contemporary conventions through a marriage between Mieszko and Rycheza, Otto III's niece, who was the daughter of the palatine Ezzo of Lower Lotharingia. This marriage also could be interpreted as a sign of Bolesław's political orientation toward establishing direct contacts with the centers of opposition to Henry within the empire.

The campaign against Rus, which was undertaken almost immediately with German and Pecheneg reinforcements, did not result in a conclusive military victory, but rather ended in a compromise which effected the release of Sviatopolk and his family from imprisonment. Because the spoils taken during the campaign were so meager, the dissatisfied Pechenegs rebelled, but Bolesław was able to suppress the revolt immediately. Probably during Bolesław's return to Poland, his army captured and occupied the region surrounding Przemyśl and Bełz, thereby securing a natural boundary and closing an easy route to Małopolska.

There was little chance that the conditions of the Peace of Merseburg would be met, because to aid Henry in his Italian campaign was obviously contrary to Poland's interests. Bolesław did not send the promised reinforcements for the Roman campaign. He was fully aware that Henry would inevitably turn against Poland after he obtained the imperial crown. Under the pretext of sending a mission to explain his procrastination, Bolesław attempted to establish ties with Henry's Lotharingian opposition, but his plan of action collapsed entirely. Bolesław's efforts to persuade Oldřich of Bohemia to the antiimperial side was also a failure. When Mieszko was entrusted with the mission to Prague, he was imprisoned and, at Henry's order, delivered to him. Only because of his father's intense efforts did the emperor finally free Mieszko, but the negotiations which led to his release only increased the friction.

Bolesław's refusal to appear before a court of Saxon princes in Merseburg to explain his actions certainly determined the outcome of Henry's decision to attack Poland. The emperor ordered his troops to assemble in July 1015 in the territory of the Dziadoszans, where both the Czech and Lutician reinforcements and the regiments of the Saxon prince Bernard were to join the army. The emperor conducted the campaign and crossed the Oder at Krosno. Prince Bernard crossed the Oder at a point further north, but the armies did not join forces because Bernard returned to Saxony after ravaging a large part of the area he had entered. Instead of coming to the aid of the emperor, the Czechs contented themselves with more local successes in Moravia. In these circumstances the emperor was forced to order a retreat, but the Poles attacked the retreating Germans and harrassed them all the way to Meissen. Though Bolesław was not able to bring Meissen under his control, he ravaged the area up to the Jahne River.

The emperor did not consider the war lost, despite his lack of success. Even though matters in Burgundy required him to remain in the west throughout 1016, he rejected all of Bolesław's overtures for a truce. He ordered another military campaign against Poland for the following summer. The situation further east had also influenced his decision. After Vladimir's death on 15 July 1015, a struggle for succession between his two sons, Sviatopolk and Jaroslav, had broken out in Kiev. It resulted in Sviatopolk's defeat, and he escaped to his father-in-law's court in Poland. Jaroslav became the emperor's natural ally and in fact signed an alliance with Henry directed against Bolesław. The emperor also gained a second ally in Stephen of Hungary. Stephen had old accounts to settle with Bolesław because of the protection he had offered to exiled rival Magyar princes, and he eagerly looked forward to this opportunity to avenge himself.

The lack of a coordinated plan of action in this alliance ruined the emperor's hopes. The Russians and Hungarians limited their hostilities to laying siege to several cities along the borders. Bolesław began the campaign in the west in June 1017, ordering the Moravians to attack the Ostmark. The Moravian diversion prevented the Bavarians from participating in the emperor's campaign against Poland. Henry was limited to his Czech and Lutician reinforcements, and together they advanced by way of Krosno to Głogów [Glogau], where Bolesław waited at the head of his troops. It is difficult to reconstruct the strategy in this campaign, because it is not clear why the emperor's army changed direction from Głogów to Kłodzko [Glatz] and along the way unsuccessfully laid siege to the city of Niemcza (Nimptsch). Because of the late season and an epidemic in the camp, the emperor decided to retreat in the direction of Bohemia.

When the emperor arrived in Merseburg on 1 October, Polish envoys soon followed with a proposal to conduct negotiations aimed at a truce and an exchange of prisoners. Henry accepted under pressure from his court. The negotiations continued for three months, but a peace was finally concluded in Budziszyn [Bautzen] on 30 January 1018. In Thietmar's words, it was not "what was desirable, but only what could be done." The emperor was indeed compelled to make a whole series of concessions. He acknowledged Bolesław's suzerainty over Moravia and upper and lower Lusatia. He agreed to send reinforcements against his own ally, Jaroslav of Rus, and he recognized Bolesław's independence from the empire. The treaty was further consolidated by a marriage between the recently widowed Bolesław and Oda, the sister of Herman, the margrave of Meissen.

Now that matters were settled in the west, Bolesław devoted his attention to affairs in Rus. He had to respond to Jaroslav's intransigent position. Jaroslav had rejected a truce in the fall of 1017 and had also refused Bolesław permission to marry his sister. With Sviatopolk still in his camp, Bolesław began his military campaign in July 1018. Jaroslav attempted to stop Bolesław's advance at the Bug, but he was roundly beaten on 22 July and had to retreat with Bolesław in close pursuit. Bolesław met little resistance in reaching the gates of Kiev and after a long siege took the city. He entered Kiev on 14 August and placed his son-in-law, Sviatopolk, on the throne.

Bolesław successfully concluded this campaign and dismissed his German, Hungarian, and Pecheneg reinforcements, while he remained in Kiev until internal affairs were normalized. His prolonged stay in Kiev and his attempts to reestablish contact with Jaroslav distressed Sviatopolk to the point that he provoked an anti-Polish revolt among the population. This forced Bolesław to withdraw from Kiev, but in an orderly fashion. Though he abandoned Kiev, during his return to Poland he captured the Grody Czerwieńskie, which Mieszko had once surrendered.

Information is rather scant regarding the events in Bolesław's reign after the Kievan campaign. It is known that he fought with minor success in Western Pomerania, which was succumbing to an increasing pagan influence exerted by the Obodorites and Luticians. Moravia was probably lost about this time (1021) and occupied by Oldřich's son, Břetislav. One of the few concrete pieces of information about Poland in the chronicles describes Bolesław's coronation.

Bolesław's efforts to obtain a crown spanned the last twenty-five years of his reign. These direct attempts began shortly after the Congress of Gniezno, when he dispatched a mission to Rome led by Abbot Astryk. The fate of that mission has already been described. Bolesław was not deterred by his lack of success and made two further attempts, in 1003 and 1004, when he commissioned a monk named Anthony to pursue his petition. These efforts failed, and Anthony was detained in Magdeburg by the Germans during his second mission and never even reached Rome. After 1005 the chronicle entries make no mention of any continuing efforts by Bolesław to petition for a crown. Perhaps the reasons were Henry's intransigent position and the fact that the emperor made every attempt to minimize the significance of Otto III's measures at the Congress of Gniezno. He strongly opposed any attempt by Bolesław to obtain a crown. Only after Henry died on 13 July 1024 and a new pope almost concurrently succeeded at Rome was Bolesław able to take advantage of disorders in the empire and reach an understanding with the new pope, John XIX. Bolesław received permission to proceed with the coronation, which finally took place on Easter Sunday, 1025.

This ceremony was enormously important. Outwardly it was a manifestation of the full sovereignty of Bolesław's state, and internally it was a symbol of its unity and indivisibility, which would rescue Bolesław's achievements from ruin during future crises.

Unfortunately, Bolesław himself was not fated to share in the benefits of his achievement. He died shortly thereafter, probably on 17 June 1025, barely fifty-seven years old. The country grieved at his death, fully realizing that, as Gall Anonim wrote, he was "the father of these lands [. . .] defender [. . .] lord; not one who ruined other's lands and possessions, but the honorable ruler of the state."

5

The Great Calamity

Bolesław was survived by his seven children from four marriages—three sons and four daughters. According to consuetudinary law, all the male heirs were entitled to share in the inheritance, which meant that both the state and the treasury were to be divided among the sons. However, Bolesław fully understood that it would pose a formidable threat to the state if several regents were to rule together. Indeed, after the death of his own father he had been forced to displace his half-brothers because the situation would have led to the dissolution of the young state Mieszko had created. Bolesław did not intend to permit a similar situation to arise again; he was determined to preserve the state from an internecine struggle and decided to break custom by transferring rule to only one heir. This decision had facilitated his obtaining a crown in 1025, since one of the most fundamental attributes of a crown is its indivisibility. According to the custom of primogeniture, the oldest son succeeded the father. Bezprym was thirty-eight years old at the time of Bolesław's death, and he was the oldest son from Bolesław's second marriage, to a Hungarian noblewoman. For unknown reasons Bolesław did not favor his oldest son's succession. Perhaps either he meant to elevate his beloved younger son or he realized that his firstborn son would not be a capable ruler. More than ten years before his death, Bolesław had begun to favor his younger son, Mieszko, as his chosen successor. He was three years younger than Bezprym, and his mother, Emnilda, was Bolesław's third wife. As Bolesław's apparent heir, Mieszko was introduced to the complexities of his father's policies and served in diplomatic missions and military campaigns. The fact that he was assigned additional responsibilities indicates that he was progressing to his father's satisfaction.

Circumstances were no less complicated after Bolesław's death than after the death of Mieszko I. Even though Mieszko II immediately succeeded his father and through his own coronation underscored his desire to continue his father's policies and defend the unity of his inherited state, he had to contend with considerable internal opposition. The opposition consisted not only of Bezprym and his supporters, who were discontented by the usurpation of the eldest son's rights, but also of Otto, the youngest son, who received only a very modest inheritance. Mieszko also had to contend with the antipathy of his stepmother, Oda, and even of his own wife, Rycheza. Rycheza was deeply offended when Mieszko began openly to favor his illegitimate son over their own son, Kazimierz, and she shifted her allegiance to the camp of Mieszko's opponents.

These difficulties did not all surface at once. On the contrary, the beginning of Mieszko's reign seemed auspicious, as Matilda, the wife of the Lotharingian prince Frederick, emphatically expressed to Mieszko in the dedication of a liturgical book. Conditions within the empire had forced Henry II's successor, Conrad II, to confront several serious obstacles. There was considerable internal opposition, such as the refusal of the king of Burgundy, Rudolph, to confer his crown on Conrad because it had been promised previously to Henry. When these matters necessitated Conrad's presence in the west, Mieszko took the opportunity to proceed with his own coronation, clearly asserting his own intention to emancipate himself from the empire. The coronation was a serious affront to the prestige of the empire in the east and, because the Polish king maintained a close relationship with the opposition camp in the empire, it created a troublesome situation for Conrad.

It was imperative that the emperor affirm his authority. However, the initiatives in this direction were not at all successful. When King Stephen of Hungary's claims as coheir to Bavaria (he was related to the prince of Bavaria through his wife) not only were rejected but the independence of Hungary was also brought into question, he too sided with the opposition camp. Mieszko quickly took advantage of the situation and formed an alliance with Stephen. In order to prevent the alliance from broadening to include Denmark, Conrad traveled to his eastern boundary, and through a series of territorial concessions attempted to dissuade Canute from entering into an alliance with Mieszko that would jeopardize the empire. He partially achieved his aim; Canute agreed only to a truce with the empire.

The greatest threat confronting Conrad was Mieszko's close relationship with the Lotharingian opposition. Any diversion Mieszko might undertake in the east in the event of a civil war in the empire could turn the tide in favor of the opposition. It was essential for Conrad to deal with this problem immediately, and in order to neutralize Mieszko, he entered into negotiations with Mieszko's two brothers. The intrigue was uncovered and the conspirators were exiled to Rus in 1026, but the situation in Poland, exacerbated by these intrigues, made it impossible for Mieszko to aid the rebellion in the empire which broke out in the fall of 1026. Perhaps Mieszko was also forced to concentrate his attention on Western Pomerania, which was being threatened by the pagan Luticians as well as by obvious signs of an imminent Danish invasion. Conrad suppressed the rebellion in the German principalities on his return from Rome, where he had been crowned emperor. This success certainly enhanced his position as emperor, and the striking proof was the fact that the matter of conferring the title of king of Burgundy on him was reconsidered in the fall of 1027. The circumstances were so significantly changed that it became obvious that all the emperor's attention would now focus on the east, particularly Poland.

After Mieszko brought matters under control in Poland, he anticipated Conrad, attacking at the border of Saxony in 1028. Mieszko felt all the more confident since the emperor's potential ally, Canute, was already engaged in a war with Norway, and Mieszko's own ally, Stephen of Hungary, was fighting the Germans on the borders of his own territories. Mieszko's campaign was in large measure successful. He ravaged a considerable area of eastern Saxony and returned with many prisoners and booty. Mieszko then turned north along the Oder in an attempt to restore his influence in Western Pomerania. He could not foresee that this action would so antagonize the Luticians that they would join the emperor's camp.

Conrad's retaliatory campaign in the following year accomplished less than he expected. It was a blundering effort; only the city of Budziszyn was besieged, and that without success.

Mieszko realized that once the war had begun in earnest it could only end with a decisive victory, and in 1030 he launched a preventive attack in the area between the Saale and Elbe rivers in order to exploit the rivalry among the Saxon pretenders to Thietmar's rule in the Ostmark. (Thietmar had died on 2 January 1030.) The Luticians joined Mieşzko in this incursion and were especially brutal in their treatment of the civilian population. Their participation in the campaign resulted in the destruction of many Christian churches.

The incursion began in February 1030 and was undertaken following King Stephen's agreement to attack the Bavarian border at the same time. The emperor decided that he would first have to deal with the Hungarians, and only after he resolved that conflict could he attack Poland. In the summer of 1030 the emperor attacked Stephen with supporting Czech troops led by Břetislav, Oldřich's son. He was not able to rout the Hungarian forces. It is rather peculiar that Mieszko did not participate in this action, leaving his Hungarian ally to his fate. The only explanation for his absence must be a diversion of some kind on Poland's eastern boundary. An entry in a Russian chronicle regarding the capture of Bełz by the Kievan prince in the same year suggests that there was a Russian encounter. It might be assumed that it was the result of Bezprym's protracted stay in Rus, and that he was able to persuade his hosts to take military action. This was all the more unsettling since both of Mieszko's exiled brothers were planning similar strategies: while Bezprym was plotting a Russian intervention, Otto was preparing an invasion plan with the Germans at the imperial court. The Russian incursion was proof of the growing threat of a simultaneous attack by Mieszko's enemies.

The situation did not become critical until 1031, when the emperor concluded a peace agreement with Stephen of Hungary and Mieszko lost his only ally. Poland was now isolated and faced the inevitability of conducting a war on two fronts, which far exceeded its capability. The imperial campaign against Poland began in fall 1031, and posed no major problems from the German point of view. Threatened by an internal revolt and attack from Rus, Mieszko was compelled to sue for peace. The conditions for peace included extraordinary demands: Mieszko was to return all the plunder taken during his previous campaign and surrender all rights to Lower Lusatia, which had been taken with so much difficulty by Bolesław Chrobry.

By agreeing to these conditions, Mieszko intended to concentrate all of his forces in the east, in order to contend with any threat of attack. The Russian princes, Jaroslav and Mstislav, had already taken the Grody Czerwieńskie, which placed the natural gateway for an attack on Poland under their control. Bezprym took advantage of these circumstances and invaded the country with Russian troops under his command. He found favorable conditions in Poland because the opposition, dissatisfied with Mieszko's politics, joined Bezprym in large numbers. In these circumstances, any further resistance was hopeless, and after a month's battle Mieszko realized that his cause was lost and fled to Bohemia. He chose Bohemia because of certain disagreements that had arisen between the emperor and Oldřich.

The victorious Bezprym took power in Poland, and a strong reaction took root against the innovations which had been introduced from abroad by previous rulers. Reaction was also directed against the young Polish church, which was largely governed by a foreign clergy. In order to maintain his position under these circumstances, Bezprym decided to break entirely with Mieszko's policies in regard to the empire. When the opportunity presented itself, Bezprym sent Conrad his brother's royal insignia and submitted himself entirely to the emperor's power.

Perhaps Rycheza, who already was at odds with her husband, accompanied the mission in order to support her son Kazimierz's interests in the negotiations between the emperor and Bezprym. One thing is certain—the emperor received his cousin graciously and granted her the right to the title of queen for the rest of her life.

Bezprym's rule lasted barely six months. The submissive attitude of the new prince in regard to the emperor rankled his previous supporters, and his despotic rule increased the numbers of the opposition. Among them was the youngest of Chrobry's sons, Otto. It was almost certainly at Otto's instigation that Bezprym was murdered. But Otto did not maintain the position that he had gained through assassination for very long, because he also was soon killed by a member of his own court.

These events transpired in less than a year from the time that Mieszko was exiled. The situation which the exiled monarch encountered on his return severely hampered his freedom of action. He came back to a state which had been enervated by the events of the previous year. The forces that sought to revert to the system of independent tribes and to overthrow the power of the Piasts had gathered strength. Mieszko could not afford a confrontation with the empire in this situation. The emperor was disturbed by the internal changes in Poland and began preparations for a military campaign, but Mieszko immediately appealed to him for a truce. An agreement was signed in Merseburg on 7 July 1032. The conditions were humiliating. Mieszko was compelled to agree to a division of the state and allow his cousin, Dietrich, to become coruler.

Mieszko had no intention of honoring conditions that were forced upon him in such difficult circumstances. When the emperor concentrated his attention on matters pertaining to the Czechs and Luticians, Mieszko forcibly united his divided state. Unfortunately, the details of how this was accomplished are not known. It certainly was not done without force, and it only multiplied the number of Mieszko's enemies. The tragic death of Chrobry's last son hardly came as a surprise. According to a twelfth-century account, he was murdered by his swordbearer on 10 May 1034.

The information, which is based on very few sources, regarding the fate of Chrobry's kingdom after the death of Mieszko II is limited and confusing. Some historians have concluded that the state passed to Mieszko's firstborn but illegitimate son, Bolesław, who ruthlessly pursued his father's enemies until they formed an alliance and assassinated him, probably in 1037.

The last of Chrobry's descendants who remained alive was Kazimierz, Mieszko and Rycheza's son. After his brother's death, he left the monastery where he had remained according to his father's wish and attempted to seize power. He was unsuccessful and escaped to the empire in the same year.

Centrifugal forces representing separatist tendencies among the tribes eventually came to dominate the state which the Piasts had been forced to abandon. The name of one of the leaders of this movement is found in the primary sources: Masław. He had been Mieszko's cupbearer and one of the most influential members of the magnate class. Perhaps he participated in the conspiracy which had planned Mieszko's and Bolesław's deaths. In the chaotic period immediately following Mieszko's death, he was able to usurp power in Mazovia and declare himself its prince. Others realized similar aims. An identical situation arose in Pomerania, which not only became politically independent but also reverted to paganism. This political revolution, which was aimed not only against the reigning dynasty but also against the knights and clergy who had upheld it, found support among the adherents of the old pagan faith in other Polish provinces. Mieszko's state became the battleground of a fierce pagan reaction, which was especially severe in Wielkopolska and Silesia. Churches and monasteries which had been built decades earlier were destroyed, their treasures stolen, and the clergy murdered. This persecution extended to secular authorities that had supported the deposed dynasty or were of foreign origin. In the conflagration that followed, the life's work of Mieszko I and Bolesław Chrobry lay in ruins.

Poland's neighbors did not fail to take advantage of the anarchic situation in the country. Břetislav had succeeded his father, Oldřich, in Bohemia in 1034 and decreed a campaign against Poland in revenge for Chrobry's previous invasion of Bohemia. When the campaign began in 1038, it met little resistance in Poland. The invaders robbed and pillaged settlements and took the inhabitants as slaves as they penetrated deep into the country. Besides taking numerous church treasures, sacred vestments, and bells, the Czechs also removed the relics of Saint Wojciech and the body of his brother, Gaudenty-Radzim, and the bodies of the Five

Martyrs. These losses were all the more serious for the church in Poland, because it had lost the sacred relics which had been of so much significance in estalishing an independent metropolitan in Gniezno. Their transfer to Prague during a period of hysterical pagan reaction in Poland easily could have contributed further to the collapse of an independent Polish church.

Břetislav did not stop merely at pillaging a defenseless Poland; during his return he occupied Silesia and annexed it to Bohemia. This event has been variously interpreted by historians. Earlier historiographers presented Břetislav as a ruler who wanted to realize the idea of a Slavic empire incorporating both Bohemia and Poland. Now this view has generally been abandoned. Poland at that time was relatively too large and densely populated to be incorporated by a much smaller Bohemia, even during this period of decline, and incorporation would have upset the internal homogeneity of both states. It is much more probable that Břetislav intended to weaken his neighbor as much as possible, and by securing his position in the north he meant to undertake the more difficult task of emancipating his country from the empire. Břetislav achieved his objective of weakening Poland by ravaging the country, depopulating the state, and annexing Silesia. Silesia now was to function as a Bohemian mark and defend the invasion routes to Moravia and Bohemia. The results of the internal unrest and the Czech invasion had tragic consequences for Poland and retarded its development by a hundred years, negating all the territorial, political, and religious gains achieved during the reigns of Mieszko I and Bolesław Chrobry.

6

The Reconstruction
of the State

Bohemia's ascendant power was contrary to German interests. As a consequence, when Kazimierz was forced into exile he was cordially received at the imperial court. Familial ties obviously played a role, since Kazimierz was related to the influential line established by Ezzo in Lotharingia and his uncle, Herman, was the archbishop of Cologne. Kazimierz's cause found powerful allies in the empire, who made every effort to restore his usurped patrimony. The court did not stop at mere expressions of sympathy, but provided Kazimierz with a detachment of five hundred men to support his return to Poland. Kazimierz probably began his campaign at the beginning of 1039. He received further support in one of the border cities from which he began his reconquest of Poland, where an inchoate situation still prevailed. Kazimierz was fortunate that he did not meet with organized resistance and, in a relatively short time, he was able to occupy a large part of Poland. Silesia remained beyond his reach and under Břetislav's control. Mazovia was ruled by Masław, and Pomerania remained fiercely opposed to the Piasts.

In the political atmosphere generated by Břetislav's policies, Kazimierz could rely on the aid and protection of the empire, but he could also safely assume that these cicumstances would not persist for long. In the event of a conflict with the empire, Kazimierz wanted to avoid being entrapped like his father, Bolesław, who had been forced to fight on two fronts. He therefore sought an alliance with Rus immediately after coming to power. The negotiations begun at his initiative were successful. Kazimierz also married Dobroniega, the sister—or, as some historians insist, the daughter—of Jaroslav, the prince of Kiev. This alliance was formed in 1039 and allowed Kazimierz to concentrate all of his forces on recouping the losses which had resulted from Břetislav's invasion.

Emperor Conrad II died on 4 June 1039 and was succeeded by Henry III, who was only twenty-one years old at the time. Henry had already been crowned king of Germany before his father's death, and over the course of several years he had been initiated into the most confidential matters of the empire. He met with no opposition when he took power and soon began to expand the empire to its heights. It required little effort on Kazimierz's part to induce Henry to oppose Břetislav, because Bohemia's strength threatened German interests, especially Czech plans to establish a metropolitan of the church in Prague. Břetislav proved himself as adept a diplomat as a military leader. Through a pretense of submission he managed to delay the threatened German invasion of 1039 for a year, using the time to prepare his country's defenses and gain a very valuable ally in the king of Hungary, Peter the Venetian [Peter Orseolo]. Břetislav had gained the support of the Hungarian king, who was in constant fear of being overthrown by the younger line of the Árpád dynasty, by expelling all the pretenders to the Hungarian throne living in Bohemia: András, Béla, and Levente. The exiled princes found protection at Kazimierz's court in Poland and participated in his campaigns to reestablish the former borders of the Piast state.

When Břetislav's stratagem became obvious, it was already too late to undertake a campaign against Bohemia until the following year. The campaign was conducted by Henry III in the summer of 1040 and ended in complete failure. The Germans were caught in an ambush that resulted in heavy losses, and they were forced to retreat from Bohemia. When news of Henry's defeat became known, the margrave of Meissen also retreated. Břetislav had received support from the Hungarians, who not only supplied him with reinforcements but also launched a diversion along the Bavarian boundary to involve part of the German force.

Henry's lack of success in the campaign of 1040 did not alter his plans. He decreed another campaign against the Czechs for the following year. On this occasion circumstances prevailed against Břetislav. He first lost his Hungarian ally because internal affairs in Hungary had brought about Peter's overthrow, and then the Germans launched an attack from a direction which Břetislav least expected. The German army was led by experienced guides through the mountains, penetrating deep into Bohemia by circumventing the border positions and passes that were defended by the Czechs. Because the bishop of Prague, Sever, and many magnates went over to the side of the opposition, Břetislav decided not to make a defensive stand at Prague and sued for peace. The conditions were extraordinary: Břetislav was to humble himself before Henry in Regensburg and swear an oath of fealty, pay an enormous fine, repay the overdue tribute, return the prisoners taken in the campaign against Poland in 1038, and compenstate the emperor and each of his princes for all losses incurred in the conflict. Accounts of the preliminary negotiations mention Poland and its losses. The opinion of certain historiographers that Kazimierz took an active part in the campaigns of 1040 and 1041, seems plausible despite the absence of information in other sources. His role served Henry's purposes, though Kazimierz did not benefit directly because he was unable to regain Silesia.

Břetislav was a competent diplomat. After arriving in Regensburg at the appointed time, he succeeded in having the harsh terms of the peace agreement ameliorated through bribes. This was achieved at the expense of one of the weakest of the co-signers, Kazimierz, who received neither any recompense for the losses suffered during the Czech invasion of 1038 nor the return of any Polish prisoners. The results of the Regensburg agreement were in full accord with German policy toward the Slavic states, which aimed at exacerbating the discontent or conflict between the states bordering the empire.

Kazimierz's petition to the Curia against Břetislav was also unsuccessful. His grievance against the Bohemian prince and Bishop Sever of Prague over the invasion of Poland and the theft of sacred church property generated much indignation at the Apostolic See, and the accused were threatened with excommunication. On the day before the verdict was announced, the Czechs were able to bribe the curial judges and, though they were not able to absolve the Czechs entirely because of the preponderance of evidence, they handed down an unusually mild sentence. The Czech prince and Bishop Sever were required to establish a monastery and provide a generous endowment as an act of expiation.

Concerted action against the Czechs was hampered in large measure by the difficulties Kazimierz faced on the Pomeranian and Mazovian borders. These difficulties were the probable cause of Kazimierz's only peripheral involvement in the Bohemian campaign of 1041. While Břetislav obtained support from the rulers of Pomerania and Mazovia in all his activities contrary to Poland's interests, Kazimierz depended on aid from Rus. Jaroslav of Kiev's invasion of Mazovia reduced the impact of Masław's diversion in 1041. Kazimierz's primary objective became the suppression of this Pomeranian and Mazovian secessionist movement. He had to secure more aid from Rus and, partly in order to achieve that end, in 1043 he gave his sister, Gertruda, in marriage to Iziaslav, Jaroslav's son.

The information in the primary sources does not provide a complete account of Kazimierz's activities. From a few fragmentary passages it appears that Kazimierz undertook a military campaign against Pomerania in 1042, which was a partial success, and then with Russian aid defeated the Mazovians in 1047. Masław was killed in the decisive battle. The Pomeranian reinforcements that were sent to aid the Mazovians against Kazimierz arrived too late and were repelled.

In analyzing the chronology of these events, Stanisław Kętrzyński proposed an interesting hypothesis regarding the date when Kazimierz regained Mazovia. He calls attention to the fact that in June 1046 the princes Břetislav of Bohemia, Kazimierz of Poland, and Ziemomysł (Zemuzil) of Pomerania appeared at the court of Henry III in Merseburg with a request that Henry arbitrate the differences between them. The German chronicler notes that the emperor settled the conflict. On this basis Kętrzyński establishes two premises: 1) that Kazimierz was at war at that time with Břetislav and his Polish allies; and 2) that one of those allies, Masław, must have been defeated before that date, because neither he nor any of his appointed delegates appeared in Meresburg. On the basis of these two premises, one could conclude that the Polish-Russian campaign against Mazovia must have taken place in the early spring of 1046, and that the false chronology which until recently remained unquestioned was the mistake of a Russian chronicler. Pursuing Kętrzyński's hypothesis, it could be assumed that the war of 1046 which ended with the fall of Masław and the defeat of the Pomeranians was a campaign in which Kazimierz fought against a coalition which also included Břetislav.

After Kazimierz reincorporated Mazovia and reestablished the suzerainty of the Piasts over Pomerania (though probably only over the eastern part), he turned his attention to the Czechs. If Kazimierz planned to attack Břetislav, he would have to keep in mind that his intention of reestablishing the Piast state along its original boundaries depended on the consent and support of the emperor. Military action against Břetislav, who had been a faithful vassal of the emperor since the Peace of Regensburg, might reverse Henry's well-disposed attitude toward Kazimierz and even threaten the process of restoration through German intervention. When Henry was absorbed by rivalries within the empire and disturbances along the Hungarian border, Kazimierz struck. The Polish campaign of 1050 caught the Czechs completely by surprise. Kazimierz was able to seize and occupy all of Silesia without much difficulty. Břetislav appealed to the emperor, who had no intention of tolerating independently undertaken political changes in the Slavic territories. Henry threatened Kazimierz with a retaliatory campaign, but a serious illness prevented him from carrying out his threat. This delay allowed Kazimierz time to appear before the emperor in Goslar in November 1050. After a grand ceremony during which Kazimierz vowed to return Silesia to Břetislav, he was returned to imperial favor.

Kazimierz did not particularly hasten to comply with his promise. Circumstances were in his favor. The emperor was so occupied, by the war with Hungary on the one hand and by the revolt of Conrad of Bavaria on the other, that he did not want to antagonize Kazimierz, who had substantial family influence in the empire. Even though Kazimierz ignored the vow he had taken in Goslar, he did not fall out of favor with the emperor, and Henry III attempted to mediate the Polish-Czech dispute in another manner. As a result of his efforts, Kazimierz and Břetislav appeared in Quedlinburg on 22 May 1054 and reached an agreement. Kazimierz was to retain Silesia, which he had seized in 1050, but he was to pay Břetislav five hundred silver and thirty gold marks per year in recompense. This agreement was an enormous diplomatic success for Kazimierz and further evidence of his increasing influence at the imperial court. It was also a clear indication of the progress Kazimierz had made in restoring the state since the time of the Czech invasion.

Details regarding the last years of Kazimierz's reign are not extant. Probably nothing of great significance took place, since the chroniclers made no entries whatsoever for the last years. This permits us to assume that Kazimierz was content with the restoration of the boundaries of the kingdom which he had originally inherited after the deaths of his father and brother.

Kazimierz did not limit himself solely to the restoration of the state; he also contributed enormously to the regeneration of the church in Poland, which had been devastated by the events of 1037 and 1038. He reestablished the ecclesiastical organization and provided the means by which the church could preserve its metropolitan in Poland.

7

Aspirations toward Greatness

The Russian and Czech method of succession convinced Kazimierz to abandon the custom originated by Chrobry, which gave the right of succession to only one heir. This process only resulted in tragic conflicts arising among all the sons. On his deathbed, Kazimierz decreed the so-called Law of the Seniorate (1058). The premise was that the elder prince would have suzerain power in the state, but that the younger members of the dynasty would inherit independent provinces within the state. Consonant with Kazimierz's decree, his oldest son, Bolesław, known by the epithets "Szczodry" [the Munificent] and "Śmiały" [the Bold], assumed suzerain power, and his two younger brothers, Władysław Herman and Mieszko, received their patrimony, though no record of where these territories were located has been preserved. Mieszko died soon after (1065), and only Władysław Herman remained as a possible heir to his brother.

Bolesław's age at the time of his father's death—he was probably no more than fifteen—required that the first years of his reign be a regency, probably directed by the widowed princess, Dobroniega. The tasks of the Polish regency were simplified thanks to the international situation at the time. After the death of Henry III on 5 October 1056, the empire underwent severe internal stresses which the regency created in the name of the adolescent Henry IV found difficult to control. After Břetislav's death on 10 January 1055, his heirs in Bohemia challenged one another for the right of succession, which entirely diverted their attention from Poland. Relations with Rus remained favorable even after Jaroslav's death in 1054. Only Hungary represented any threat. King András, who had ruled since 1046, in 1056 declared his son, Salamon, his heir and announced his son's betrothal to Henry III's sister, Judith, contrary to an agreement he had made with his brother, Béla. This decision erased all of Béla's hopes and caused the embittered prince to take asylum at the favorably disposed Polish court, but the result was a marked chill in Polish–Hungarian relations. Yet despite this irritation between Hungary and Poland, the general international situation after Kazimierz's death was so auspicious that the moment of succession did not prove to be difficult. The conduct of state affairs during the regency period could actually be considered a continuation of Kazimierz's reign. It was characterized by an emphasis on the restoration of the church, especially the reconstruction of the churches in the bishoprics which had been destroyed during the incursions of 1037 and 1038, and the return of the archbishopric to Gniezno, because for a time it had been transferred to Kraków.

A presentiment of further complications which would reorient Poland's interests toward the south was the support Béla received in his struggle with András. The fact that Hungary was drawing closer to the imperial camp was a serious threat to Poland. It was all the more serious because András's son-in-law, the ambitious young Czech prince Vratislav, was anxious to assume power in Bohemia. It was probably this very fact that inclined Poland to involve itself directly in the events that were to follow. The exiled Béla returned to Hungary with Polish reinforcements, and, after a battle in which András was killed, he took power in 1061. Salamon and Judith were forced to escape and seek refuge at the imperial court.

The support that Béla had received from Poland was an affront to the prestige and interests of the empire and a foreshadowing of the complications which would arise in Polish–German relations. There were also other reasons causing an even more clearly defined conflict. When Bolesław came of age he assumed complete power in the state. He had many noble attributes—he was courageous and valiant in battle and famous for his generosity—but he was also known for his uncontrollable temper, arrogance, and rashness, which at times made him act without fully taking into account the possible consequences. A young monarch with these character traits would not content himself with grey, everyday matters, but would aspire to the glory and greatness which he saw in the example of his splendid great-grandfather, Bolesław Chrobry. His great ambitions demanded experience and maturity in military and political affairs, but Bolesław had neither, and most of all he lacked the patience to strive toward his objective. Despite his clear successes, he not only failed to expand the territory of his state but even lost some of the gains his father had achieved.

By the time Bolesław assumed suzerain power in Poland, Vratislav of Bohemia had also come to power (February 1061). Bolesław regarded Vratislav as a natural enemy of his own ally, Béla, and he began to encourage younger pretenders to the Bohemian throne. He also refused to pay the tribute for Silesia which was due the Czechs according to the agreement of 1054, and in the summer of 1061, he led a military campaign against Vratislav. The campaign indicated Bolesław's lack of foresight: while laying siege to Hradec in Moravia, he was caught by surprise and forced to retreat quickly.

In the empire the matter of the exiled prince Salamon had again been taken up. Though the regency's intervention in 1062 had failed, the second campaign in the following year under the leadership of young Henry IV was a complete success. The empire succeeded in placing Salamon on the Hungarian throne, and since Béla died at approximately the same time, Salamon returned without a struggle and forced his cousins into exile.

The rather sketchy information in the primary sources does not indicate whether the Poles aided Béla. To the contrary, an entry for the year 1063 indicates that there was an improvement in Polish-Czech relations, which was sealed by a marriage between the widowed Vratislav and Bolesław Śmiały's sister, Świętosława. This rather odd attempt to arrange an agreement with a recent foe and devoted servant of the empire at the very moment when Poland's own ally had to contend with a foreign intervention perhaps could be interpreted merely as the result of a desire to neutralize the Czechs and prevent their aiding the empire in its conflict with Hungary. If that was the intent of the agreement, then it was a complete success, because the Czechs did not send any reinforcements in the imperial campaign against Hungary in 1063.

There is additional proof to support the validity of this view. In the following year, Poland gave aid to Béla's son, Géza, who returned to Hungary and won an independent province which had been under Béla's control during András's reign.

The fact that Bolesław had concentrated all of his attention on the south reflected a careless indifference toward the other boundaries. A pagan reaction had swept the land of the Obodrites in 1066, and from there the revolt took on both a religious and a national character and spread through the remaining Polabian tribes to the Polish border. The barely pacified Pomeranian region rebelled and broke away from the Piast rule reestablished by Kazimierz. Concurrent with the political upheaval, a pagan reaction began, which resulted in the collapse of the church in the area for the second time. The sequence of events that followed went unrecorded, and there is no explanation why Bolesław Śmiały, though he aspired to Chrobry's greatness, was so easily reconciled to the loss of Pomerania and never attempted to regain this province. It was certainly not because he lacked military strength; Bolesław's power was evident from his course of action in other areas.

When Iziaslav Jaroslavovich, who was married to Mieszko II's daughter, Gertruda, was exiled from Kiev and arrived in Poland in 1069, Bolesław did not reject his request for aid, but led a military campaign that restored Iziaslav to the throne.

Bolesław's aggressive policy in relation to Bohemia was proof of his military capability. Exploiting the family discord among the Czech princes, Bolesław annulled the agreement signed in 1063 and began a series of annual incursions into Bohemia. The first campaign was undertaken in 1071. Henry IV was disturbed by Bolesław's actions and demanded that the quarreling parties appear before him in Meissen, threatening the one who would first raise arms against the other with his disfavor. Bolesław must have been confident of his strength, because he obviously not only took the emperor's threat lightly when he invaded Bohemia again in 1072, but he also refused to pay the tribute due the empire since the capitulation of Mieszko II. His behavior was meant to provoke the empire, and in August 1073, Henry IV called for a campaign against Poland. The campaign was never organized because the Saxon lords, who had been at odds with the emperor for some time, seized the occasion to rebel against him. In a short time the entire northern part of the empire was in revolt.

The Saxon revolt postponed the confrontation between Bolesław and the empire. The danger of an invasion was in no way alleviated, and Bolesław methodically prepared for the inevitable campaign. He had to avoid the risk of a war on two fronts, and after Iziaslav was exiled from Kiev a second time in 1073, Bolesław signed a truce with his brother, Sviatoslav (1074). Without any hope of Polish intervention, Iziaslav left Bolesław's court to seek aid in the empire.

The Saxon revolt also influenced matters in the Hungarian upheaval, for Géza in 1074 took advantage of Henry's difficulties and challenged and won Salamon's crown. The exiled Salamon took refuge at his brother-in-law's court in the empire, and, in order to induce the emperor to take a greater interest in his fate, he took the oath of a vassal. Through this act he was able to secure Henry's aid. However, the imperial campaign which was to have restored Salamon to the throne ended in a complete fiasco.

Bolesław took the initiative. He fully realized that war with the empire was inevitable and hurried to exploit the civil war within it in order to weaken his opponent. In 1075 he undertook a campaign against Henry who was still fighting the Saxons. In the following year Bolesław attacked the empire's faithful vassal, Vratislav. Henry was forced to retreat from Saxony, and Vratislav abandoned Meissen, which he had recently occupied.

Bolesław also attempted to establish relations with Henry's enemies, both in the empire and outside. This policy certainly caused Bolesław to establish closer ties with Pope Gregory VII, who had been elected on 22 April 1073. Gregory was well known even during the reigns of his predecessors as an uncompromising proponent of church reforms and an opponent of those privileges in matters of church organization which served secular interests. Gregory's views opposed the interests of the German kings, who had most effectively exercised their power in church matters for purely secular ends. Gregory VII desired to free the church from injurious secular pressures, and Henry's political enemies meant to weaken his political power. The two sought a mutual understanding. Bolesław Śmiały had one further reason inducing him to negotiate with the Apostolic See. If he could obtain a crown, it would bear witness to Poland's complete emancipation from German influence and continue the tradition which Chrobry had established. These reasons inclined Bolesław to create a firm bond with the reform camp of the church and to agree to submit the Gniezno metropolitan to the Gregorian reform.

As a result, papal legates arrived in Poland in 1075 to discuss the specifics of the reforms. Negotiations pertaining to the coronation were conducted in Rome, and many difficulties had to be overcome. It is conceivable that the pope's break with Henry IV influenced his final decision, because Bolesław's coronation took place toward the end of 1076, between the time when Henry was excommunicated and his humiliation at Canossa.

Bolesław's magnificent coronation took place on 25 December 1076. Fifteen bishops assisted, and unless the chronicler made a mistake, members of another episcopate must have been present, because Poland did not have that many bishoprics at that time. Perhaps the legates previously sent by the pope participated in the ceremony.

Bolesław Śmiały's coronation sent tremors through the empire, just as Bolesław Chrobry's had done. Outraged voices were raised against this vassal who had dared to declare his independence. The indignation was all the greater because an ally of the Gregorian camp had secured a crown.

Bolesław's coronation also provoked a strong reaction in Poland. The seniorate system that had been established by Kazimierz would be replaced by primogeniture in the dynastic line and establish the indivisibility of the Piast inheritance, now a kingdom.

This was clearly contrary to the interests of the junior member, Władysław Herman, who was deprived of almost any chance to rule Poland. To an even greater degree, it went contrary to the decentralization preferred by the families of the magnate class. The magnates were in large part descendants of past tribal dynasties who had been deprived of their independent standing by the Piasts, but when Chrobry's state had collapsed they again returned to power. Kazimierz's restoration of the dynasty must have depended on some kind of compromise with this magnate class. The magnates did not want to lose any of the privileges they had gained. Their greatest enemy had always been autocratic rule, and if they agreed to be ruled by a monarch, then they would prefer to have him at his weakest. Perhaps it was due to pressure from the magnates that Kazimierz had established the seniorate, through which the power of the prince had been considerably weakened. With Bolesław elevated to a monarch, the magnates felt threatened. The autocratic rule of a king known for his irascibility was bound not only to result in the loss of those privileges already attained, but also could threaten the magnates' independent status. They represented an opposing faction which Henry IV was able to manipulate effectively to overthrow his obstinate enemy.

Bolesław was at the height of his success. When Géza died in April 1077 and Hungary was threatened by Salamon's return, Bolesław succeeded in placing Géza's brother, László, on the throne despite an incursion by the Czechs. The same year, at the request of the Apostolic See, Bolesław sent reinforcements to Iziaslav and placed him on the throne of Kiev, which was without an heir after the death of Sviatoslav. He was able to accomplish this because his chief opponent, Henry IV, was involved in a life-and-death struggle with the imperial opposition led by the antiking, Rudolph.

Because Poland's military forces were widely dispersed, Bolesław's enemies finally gained the advantage. Foremost among them was the new chancellor of the empire, the bishop of Prague, Jaromír-Gebhard, who knew Bolesław well. The opposition in Poland coalesced with the support of foreign factions. Its members consisted of the magnates who were dissatisfied with the increased power of the monarch, the Polish opponents of church reform, and the supporters of the disenfranchised younger brother, Władysław Herman. It is very doubtful whether this passive and vacillating younger brother could have initiated the planned coup d'état.

The complete history of this conspiracy is unknown, and we can determine a course of events only on the basis of Gall Anonim's account, which leaves much unsaid. The chronicler's entry reads:

> One could say much of how King Bolesław was exiled from Poland, but it should be said that the anointed should never seek corporal revenge against the anointed, for it is a sin. It harmed him greatly when he traded sin for sin by severing the members of the bishop's body for his act of treason. We do not justify the bishop's treason, nor do we recommend the vile vengefulness of the king, but let us stop here in the middle and describe how the king was received in Hungary.

That is all the chronicler entered.

There are few texts in Polish historiography which give rise to so many different explanations and evoke such impassioned debate. Only one thing is certain, and that is that we have not gone beyond conjecture. The most widely accepted view is the following. The conspiracy which certainly formed by 1078 probably led to an armed insurrection by the beginning of the following year. The conspirators were supported by Vratislav of Bohemia. Meanwhile, Henry IV led a campaign against Hungary in order to prevent László from sending aid to Bolesław. Bolesław still managed some initial successes. Bishop Stanisław of Kraków, a member of the conspiracy, was captured. The king's rash decision in ordering the bishop's execution and dismemberment on 11 April 1079 did not frighten and disorganize his opponents; it only increased their numbers. Bolesław could no longer resist the mounting pressure, and he escaped to Hungary with the hope that he would be able to obtain reinforcements from László and return to Poland.

Fate determined otherwise. Before he could obtain Hungarian aid, Bolesław died in mysterious circumstances. He most probably died very soon after beginning his exile at the hands of assassins sent by the conspirators in Poland. Only his quick death would explain the fact that he made no effort to regain the throne.

8

Rule of the Magnates

After the conspirators' victory, a choice had to be made whether to depose the Piast dynasty altogether or place one of its members on the throne. The latter course was taken because the first would easily lead to disastrous conflicts between rival members of the magnate class. There were only two possible candidates among the Piasts: Bolesław's young son, Mieszko, and Bolesław's brother, Władysław Herman. Mieszko's candidacy was out of the question because of what his father had represented. Only Władysław Herman remained, whose weak and vacillating nature was the best guarantee that he would not attempt to bolster the authority of the prince, but rather pass full power over to the hands of the victorious magnate class. That is precisely what happened, and within a short time the state was being directed by the palatine and wojewoda, Sieciech. As a descendant of the sovereign princes of Tyniec and one of the principal members of the conspiracy against Bolesław, Sieciech had ambitions to become the ruler of the state and perhaps even ultimately to replace the Piast dynasty. His position was comparable to that of the powerful major domus at the Merovingian court.

Władysław Herman was compelled to alter Poland's foreign policy radically in order to assume the throne. He broke with the Gregorian reform camp, renounced all aspirations toward emancipation from the empire, severed friendly ties with Hungary, and moved toward closer cooperation with Bohemia. The fact that Władysław never had any dynastic ambitions and had only lived in concubinage permitted the Czech-Polish agreement to be sealed by a marriage between him and Judyta, the sister of a Czech prince, in 1080.

The first years of Władysław Herman's rule were sketchily recorded, though relations with Bohemia did worsen after Henry IV designated Vratislav king of Bohemia and Poland in 1085. This title probably meant that Vratislav had the right of succession in Poland after the death of Władysław Herman, who had no male heir at the time. Władysław reacted quickly to the danger represented by a possible Czech succession. He improved relations with Hungary and recalled Bolesław's son, Mieszko, from exile (1086). It is difficult to say what motivated Władysław Herman: whether it was to counter Vratislav with the presence of a rightful heir to the Polish throne or simply familial affection.

When it became apparent that Henry had no intention of supporting Czech aspirations to annex Polish territories and when Władysław Herman's long-awaited heir, Bolesław, was born in the autumn of 1086, there was a return to a pro-German posture in Polish policy. A major role was played by the faction whose goal was to create a strong bond between Władysław Herman and the emperor, which resulted in a marriage between the now widowed Władysław and Henry IV's sister, Judyta, who had also been widowed after the death of the Hungarian king, Salamon.

The return of Bolesław Śmiały's son to Poland antagonized the members of the old conspiracy. Their fears were due to the increasing popularity of the young prince. According to the still valid law of the seniorate, Mieszko would be next in succession after the death of Władysław Herman, and the members of the conspiracy had reason to fear that Bolesław's son would seek revenge. These circumstances led them to assassinate the young prince. Gall Anonim was well aware of the events and wrote, "It is said that certain rivals, fearful that he would avenge his father, poisoned the boy of great talents, and those who were drinking with him barely escaped death." Mieszko was assassinated in 1089, without doubt at the hands of the same men who had exiled his father. It is most probable that Sieciech was involved in the assassination.

In effect, Sieciech was the real ruler of Poland and, with little deference to the weak-willed Władysław Herman, he became a virtual despot. Gall Anonim laments, "He did many cruel and intolerable things. For no good reason he sold men into slavery;

others he exiled from the country and elevated men of low rank above those nobly born." This clever and handsome palatine was able to gain favor with the prince's second wife, Judyta, and with her help they completely manipulated the undiscerning Władysław Herman. On Sieciech's advice Władysław Herman sent his illegitimate son, Zbigniew, who had been living in Kraków, to a monastery in Saxony. This banishment caused further discontent among those who interpreted it as a step taken by the powerful palatine to overthrow the Piast dynasty, but Sieciech dealt severely and ruthlessly with any sign of opposition. Whatever the repressions and persecutions, however, the ferment in the country could not be suppressed. The numerous groups that had been persecuted into leaving the country had thoughts only of revenge. In order to turn the opposition's attention in another direction, in the summer of 1090, Sieciech organized a campaign against the Pomeranian region of the Vistula basin and was able to occupy a large section of that territory. Troops were garrisoned there, and the larger settlements were burned so that they could not become rallying points for a revolt, but this tactic could not prevent an uprising that swept away the undermanned garrisons and then carried over to the left bank of the Noteć [Netze]. The retaliatory campaign which was undertaken the following year failed completely. The attempt to take the city of Nakło [Nakel] with the aid of Czech reinforcements also failed.

The Poles who had been exiled to Bohemia for political reasons reestablished ties with Poland and, after abducting Zbigniew from the monastery, attacked Silesia. They were benevolently received by the castellan of Wrocław, Magnus, who agreed to act as Zbigniew's guardian and became his official spokesman. The Czechs gave their support to the exiles.

Władysław Herman's situation was especially difficult, because all his attempts to reach an understanding with the Silesian nobility had failed. The only alternative was to use force. The campaign against Silesia was undertaken with aid of Hungarian troops, but it took a peculiar turn. In order to avenge the deaths of Bolesław Śmiały and his son Mieszko, the Hungarian king, László, entered the Polish camp and seized both the wojewoda

Sieciech and Władysław Herman's son, Bolesław Krzywousty [Wrymouth]. To continue the campaign under these circumstances was impossible, and Władysław Herman was forced to concede. Under pressure he declared Zbigniew his legitimate son and sanctioned his continued residence in Silesia (1093).

The peace proved short-lived. Sieciech managed to escape from Hungary and began to incite a reaction against Zbigniew. The ties which Sieciech established with the Silesian magnates permitted Władysław Herman to undertake a new campaign against Zbigniew with the aim of invalidating the act of legitimacy and thereby disinheriting him. Zbigniew now could not depend on the aid of the Silesian nobility and, abandoned by his previous supporters, he escaped to Kujavia, which had declared itself for him. Despite aid from Pomerania, the Kujavians were defeated, which forced Zbigniew to capitulate. He surrendered to his father, who had guaranteed his personal safety, but he became a prisoner under Sieciech's personal supervision and remained at his castle for many years. In 1097, Władysław finally granted Zbigniew his freedom and all due rights as his son as a concession to the demands of the magnates opposed to Sieciech.

Sieciech's activities, which only the myopic Władysław Herman was unable to perceive, caused growing concern about the safety of the young Piasts. Zbigniew and his younger brother, Bolesław Krzywousty, drew closer together. The two princes decided to make a common stand in defense of their rights and demanded that their father transfer his power to them. Władysław Herman acceded to the demands of his sons, who had the allegiance of the supporters of the dynasty. The state was divided into two parts, with Zbigniew inheriting Wielkopolska, Kujavia, Sieradz, and Łęczyca. Bolesław received Małopolska, Silesia, Lubusz, and a small area in western Wielkopolska. For the time being Władysław Herman retained Mazovia, which was to pass to Zbigniew after his death, and control over the major cities in Bolesław's inheritance. This agreement did not mention Sieciech's removal, and the results of this oversight soon followed, because the wojewoda entered into intrigues aimed at negating the recently concluded agreement. Gall Anonim further noted:

Sieciech . . . set many traps for both young men and through various machinations turned the father's heart and mind away from his sons. In the cities that were granted to the young princes, he placed administrators and stewards from his own family or men of lower station. They were subject to the young princes, but [Sieciech] inclined them through his perfidious cunning to be disobedient.

Sieciech's intent to destroy the Piast dynasty was obvious, and the young princes were exhorted to protect themselves against the palatine. When Bolesław's father ordered him to wage a campaign against the Czechs and the circumstances under which the campaign was to take place made him suspicious that an attempt would be made on his life, an open break occurred between the sons and the father. The brothers called for an assembly in Wrocław, where they presented the dangers that threatened them through Sieciech's plotting. They received the full support of the assembly, which was prepared to go into battle against Władysław Herman in order to overthrow the all-too-powerful palatine. News of this decision reached Władysław Herman, and both sides feverishly began to make plans for war. Gall Anonim described the events that followed.

Władysław Herman and his sons took up positions with their armies in a place known as Żarnowiec [on the river Pilica]—the sons divided against the father. There they continued their negotiations for a long time until the sons finally convinced their father, through the influence of dignitaries and their own threats, to abandon Sieciech. It is said the father also pledged to the sons that he would never allow Sieciech to regain his previous rank. When Sieciech returned to the city which bears his name [Sieciechów on the Vistula near Dęblin], the brothers came before their father humbly, calmly, and without weapons, and offered him their devotion, not as independent princes, but with bowed heads as knights [vassals] and his subjects. Then the father and the sons and all the nobles, now united, together with the whole army followed in pursuit of Sieciech, who had fled to the city which he himself had built. As they pursued him and attempted to force him to flee the country, the prince himself, when it was thought that he was sound asleep and without the knowledge of anyone but three of his most devoted confidants, quietly left the camp and crossed the Vistula by boat in order to reach Sieciech. All the nobility were outraged and declared that to abandon his sons and so many nobles and the army is not a rational man's decision, but a madman's choice. Immediately an assembly was called, and it was decided that Bolesław should take Sandomierz and Kraków, the largest and nearest seats of the kingdom, and he accepted their vows of fealty that they would be subject to his rule. Zbigniew was to hurry to Mazovia and take the city of Płock and the surrounding area. Bolesław did indeed take and rule the named cities, but Zbigniew was intercepted by his father and did not achieve what he intended.[. . .] And after a time the sons assembled the nobles and an army and made camp on the opposite shore of the Vistula from Płock, and the Archbishop Marcin, a faithful elder with great foresight, ameliorated the anger and disagreement, but with difficulty, between the father and the sons. Prince Władysław, it is said, reaffirmed his vow never again to take the side of Sieciech. Then Bolesław returned all the capitals that had been seized to his father, but his father did not keep to the agreement with his sons. But finally the sons forced the father to exile Sieciech from Poland and thereby satisfy their demands.

The chronicler adds that the powerful palatine returned to Poland from exile but remains silent concerning his further fate, only commenting that he never regained his previous influence. Perhaps he met with the punishment often meted out for acts against the state: blinding.

Sieciech had in effect attempted to strengthen ducal power, though he was motivated only by self-interest. His fall was a significant stage in the magnates' struggle against ducal power. The vacant office of palatine was not filled until after the death of Władysław Herman.

One more point should be noted regarding a further stage in the magnates' struggle against the Piast dynasty. Contrary to established tradition, Władysław Herman chose not to designate a *princeps* or senior prince on his deathbed, which left both sons with equal shares of power. This was tantamount to further weakening ducal power because, in essence, the state was divided into two equivalent provinces. Only the magnates could benefit from such a situation.

9

Access to the
Baltic Sea

After Władysław Herman's death on 4 June 1102, a rivalry emerged between his two sons that would grow more intense. It began literally at their father's funeral over the division of Władysław's lands and his treasury. The dispute was mediated by Archbishop Marcin, who settled the differences between the arguing brothers. Zbigniew received Mazovia and Płock and perhaps Kraków as well, while Bolesław received Sandomierz and Wrocław. Because neither brother had inherited the rights of senior prince, Poland in effect was split into two separate provinces.

The two brothers represented a considerable contrast in terms of personality and character. The older Zbigniew had a calm disposition and preferred to avoid armed conflict. He strove to maintain good relations with his neighbors and was inclined to use diplomacy with his enemies rather than belligerent confrontation. The younger Bolesław was his complete opposite. He enthusiastically participated in the training exercises of the court knights, and as a young man he actively joined military campaigns, which brought him recognition and popularity among the knights. He was especially eager for campaigns against the rich Pomeranian areas of the Oder basin. In this respect Bolesław represented the old Piast aspirations of annexing this territory to the Polish state.

But the realization of such aspirations would first require that Bolesław resolve the problem of the division of the Polish state into two rival provinces. Very early in his reign, Bolesław began to seek allies for the inevitable confrontation with his brother. By marrying Zbysława, the daughter of the grand prince of Kiev, in 1103, he also formed an alliance with her brother, Jaroslav of Volynia. There was little doubt in regard to the aims of his alliance. Zbigniew reacted by concluding agreements with the Czechs, the Pomeranians, and perhaps even with the empire. He then incited the Czechs and Pomeranians to attack Bolesław's territories, which were severely ravaged. Krzywousty was forced to conduct a war on two fronts, which effectively contained his expansionist ambitions. The most serious threat was the possibility of German intervention. In order to protect himself from this eventuality, Bolesław signed an agreement with the Hungarian king, Kálmán, "that if the emperor should lead an incursion into either one of their lands, then the other shall hold the Czechs at bay" (Gall Anonim). He also attempted to find a basis of agreement with the Apostolic See, which was inimically disposed toward the empire and the Czechs.

Despite these circumstances, Bolesław attempted to formulate some kind of agreement with Zbigniew in regard to Pomerania. As Gall Anonim reported, in 1106 they even came to an understanding that "one without the other will not enter into agreements with enemies, whether in regard to war or peace, nor will one without the other enter into any alliance, and that one will aid the other against his enemies and provide all necessary aid."

Zbigniew did not honor the agreement, and when Bolesław undertook a new campaign against Pomerania, he not only refused to aid his brother, but even sent his army to turn back Bolesław's forces from the Pomeranian border. His reasons were undoubtedly a desire to protect his own lands from the aftermath of such a conflict and to maintain friendly ties with the Pomeranians. Relations between the brothers inevitably led to a major confrontation. Both anxiously made certain that they could depend on the help of their allies: Zbigniew relied on the Pomeranians and Czechs, while Bolesław depended on Hungary and Rus. Bolesław acted quickly and struck first against his brother after convincing the Czechs not to intervene. He attacked Zbigniew with full force and occupied the cities of Kalisz, Gniezno, Spicymierz, and Łęczyca. When he later obtained Hungarian and Russian reinforcements, Bolesław attacked his brother in Mazovia. All that the defeated Zbigniew could do was humble himself before his brother and acknowledge his suzerainty.

Zbigniew's defeat meant a considerable loss in the territory of his patrimony. Bolesław left him only Mazovia, and as a fief, not an independent principality.

In order to avenge himself on the Pomeranians for aiding Zbigniew, Bolesław attacked Białogród [Belgard] and Kołobrzeg in the winter of 1107. The campaign was a success, and the area became a Polish fief. These events contributed further to the conflict between the brothers because, contrary to his obligation as a vassal, Zbigniew did not send reinforcements. This breach of duty caused Bolesław to take strong action. Gall Anonim described the events that followed.

> Realizing that his brother did not honor any of those things to which he had pledged and vowed and that he was a hindrance to the entire country because he was dangerous and guilty, Bolesław expelled him from all the lands of the Polish kingdom, and with the aid of those who supported [Zbigniew] and defended the city on the borders of the state, he defeated the Hungarians and Russians.

The exiled Zbigniew sought sanctuary and aid in Bohemia and the empire.

Zbigniew's expulsion permitted Bolesław to undertake a systematic expansion toward the sea, a movement which up until this time had been repeatedly interrupted because of domestic problems. Krzywousty still required a stronger military force to conduct his campaign and to secure bases of operation on the Noteć and Vistula. He could then concentrate his attack on both central Pomerania and the area of the Vistula basin. A campaign was launched against the cities which defended the access routes through the swamps of the Noteć area, and pitched battles were fought with fluctuating success. The Pomeranians penetrated deep into Bolesław's territories several times, and during one such incursion nearly captured Archbishop Marcin. Krzywousty retaliated in kind. With Mazovia under his control, he broadened his plan of annexing the coastal area by expanding his attack to include the lands inhabited by the Prussians, whom he first attacked in winter 1107.

The Pomeranians fully realized the extent of the danger which would threaten them if the Poles were able to seize the access routes through the Noteć swamps. For this reason they could not limit their strategy to defensive maneuvers; they had to take the offensive at the first opportunity. That occurred when Bolesław, according to an agreement with the Hungarian king, Kálmán, was obliged to undertake a diversion against the Czechs after the Germans attacked Hungary in the fall of 1108. The Pomeranians exploited the opportunity and, aided by an act of treason, took the city of Ujście [Usch]. Bolesław rushed back to retaliate. That did not restrain the Pomeranians from continuing their attack the following year or from entering into an alliance with the Czechs, which included the objective of returning Zbigniew to power. Both the Czech attack on Silesia and the concurrent Pomeranian attack on Mazovia were repelled.

These events inclined Bolesław to take more drastic action. The city of Nakło, which was strategically very important in the Pomeranian line of defense along the Noteć, was surrounded by Polish troops in summer 1109. The city stubbornly defended itself while a very large relief column of a united Pomeranian force hurried to Nakło. Polish detachments encountered the Pomeranians on 10 August, and in the decisive battle that followed the Pomeranians were completely routed. This sealed the fate of Nakło and six other cities—probably the entire region known as the Kraina—which were forced to capitulate. Bolesław was not able fully to exploit his military advantage at the moment when he occupied these cities, because a German invasion now threatened Poland.

In revenge for the unsuccessful campaign against Hungary in the previous year, which had been frustrated by Bolesław's effective diversionary tactics against the Czechs, Henry V marched to the Polish border. According to Gall Anonim, Henry sent the following ultimatum to the Polish prince before any confrontation took place. "Either you agree to accept your brother, give him half the kingdom, and pay me either three hundred marks yearly in tribute or send me three hundred knights for my campaign, or the alternative is to divide your kingdom with me by the sword—if you are able."

Bolesław's answer was very characteristic. He completely rejected any possibility of Polish dependence upon the empire, which would have obliged him to lend Henry military support as well as submit to Henry's courts in purely internal matters. He agreed instead to give military or financial aid to the Roman Catholic church, with Henry as intermediary and *advocatus* for the Apostolic See. Such a concept of Polish-German relations was completely unacceptable from the German point of view. The matter predictably resulted in a major German-Czech campaign launched against Poland in August 1109. It forced Bolesław to make concessions in the north and made it impossible for him to annex the Kraina. This territory became a vassal state under the control of a distant cousin of the Piasts, Świętopełk, the ruler in the Vistula basin of Pomerania.

The German-Czech forces invaded Silesia but were unable to take the stubbornly defended city of Lower Bytom [Beuthen]. They were forced to move north toward Głogów, where they managed finally to cross over to the right bank of the Oder. Głogów was defended as valiantly as Bytom had been. Henry launched an attack against Wrocław, but again met with stiff opposition. Bolesław used guerilla tactics to weaken the invading army, demoralizing it and causing significant losses. Gall Anonim described the difficulties with which Henry contended in a most animated way.

> The emperor realized that all his might, his gifts, and his promises had proved themselves useless against the inhabitants [of Głogów] and that remaining there any longer would accomplish nothing. After taking counsel he marched against the city of Wrocław, but there too he still had to reckon with Bolesław's military talent and strength. Wherever the emperor marched or stopped to make camp, Bolesław followed at a distance, but remained near the place where the emperor camped. And when the emperor prepared to continue and broke camp, Bolesław was there just as an inseparable companion during the march; and if anyone dared to step out of formation, then he would not find his way back; and if a detachment, confident in its number, separated in order to search for supplies or fodder for the horses, then Bolesław would immediately attack them in the center and cut off their retreat. And so the emperor's army that had come after plunder was itself plundered by Bolesław. By these means he drove so large and fine an army to the point of such fear that even the Czechs, who are born plunder-

ers, were forced to exist on their own supplies or go hungry, because no one dared leave the camp; no squire attempted to gather grasses for the horses, nor did anyone even dare to go beyond the guardposts to relieve their bodily functions. They were in fear of Bolesław day and night; reminding one another that Bolesław does not sleep; [he was] always on their minds. When they approached a thicket or bosk, they shouted, "Be careful, Bolesław is there." There was not a place where they did not believe Bolesław was hiding. He ceaselessly harassed them in their way, cutting off several of them from the front of the formation, sometimes from the rear and other times from the sides. That is why each of the emperor's soldiers marched all day long fully equipped, expecting Bolesław to appear anywhere and at any time. At night they slept in their armor or stood at their posts; some spent the night walking the camp in a circle; others shouted, "Be alert, be vigilant, be careful"; and finally others sang a song about Bolesław's courage.

Under these conditions Henry attempted to reach an agreement. He abandoned Zbigniew's cause and limited his demands to the payment of a tribute, but Krzywousty rejected this offer as well. Because his siege of Wrocław ended in failure, Henry ordered a retreat. On 21 September 1109, during the retreat, the Czech prince, Svatopluk, was assassinated in the camp by a member of the house of Vršovec in revenge for the wrongs committed against his family.

Folk imagination in time exaggerated Bolesław's success and created a legend about the German defeat at Psie Pole.

Henry's failure now permitted Krzywousty to take the initiative and wage a campaign against Bohemia. Its objectives were to take revenge for Czech support of the German invasion and to place Bořivoj, who had been Svatopluk's archfoe, on the throne. Bořivoj was not able to maintain the position which he had gained through Polish assistance, and he fell into German hands after he was exiled by his brother Vladislav. Bolesław now supported a new pretender to the throne, Bořivoj's youngest brother, Soběslav. With this objective in mind, a campaign against Bohemia was launched that ended in a splendid victory for the Poles at the River Trutina on 8 October 1110, and after the negotiations that followed, a peace agreement was finalized in 1111. Both sides agreed to accept the return and adequately enfranchise in their own countries the exiled pretenders to their respective thrones, while also agreeing not to support domestic dissension in neighboring states.

In accord with the agreement, the exiled Zbigniew returned to Poland. On his brother's orders he was blinded and soon after died. Gall Anonim did not hesitate to censure Bolesław's deed as a pitiful crime and sin. He presented the motives which led Krzywousty to commit fratricide.

> Zbigniew followed the advice of foolish people, not mindful of his pledge of humility and submission, and came to Bolesław not as a humble man, but as a defiant one, not as it befitted a remorseful man after a long exile, exhausted by hardships and lack of success, but rather independent-minded, ordering a sword to be carried in front of him among an orchestra of musicians beating on drums and playing zithers, and exhibiting the air of a sovereign and not a subject, who had intentions not so much to submit to his brother's orders, but himself to order his brother. Certain sensible people interpreted this in a way that even Zbigniew had not intended, and gave Bolesław such advice that, because he believed it, immediately made him grieve and will always make him grieve for what he did. Such were the words that turned his mind: "This man who was crushed by so many defeats and exiled for so long, now when he first appears again, even though he is not certain under what exact conditions, arrives proud and with such pomp—what will he do in the future if any power is given to him in Poland?" They also added other more menacing information, namely that Zbigniew already had found and arranged for someone from a certain wealthy or impoverished family to stab Bolesław with a knife or some other steel object.

It is difficult to determine whether these were his real motives or whether there were others that prompted Bolesław to act. One thing is certain: by this crime Bolesław rid himself of an inconvenient rival who hampered his freedom of action, especially in regard to Pomerania.

At the time Pomerania demanded increased attention, because Świętopełk took advantage of the German invasion and the period of the Czech wars in order to renounce his vassal's oath. As long as Bolesław was occupied in the south, it was difficult for him to react forcefully, and he was restricted to minor incursions into

Pomerania and the Prussian area. Only after Bolesław concluded a peace agreement with the Czechs was he able to conduct a full-scale war against Świętopełk. The siege of Nakło that began in the fall of 1112 ended in a fiasco. Indeed, Świętopełk promised to pay a tribute and even surrendered his own son as a hostage, but he never kept to the agreement, and he forced Bolesław to undertake a new campaign the following year. On this occasion the results were much more favorable. Bolesław took Wyszogród [Wiesse-grad] on the Vistula, perhaps Świecie [Schwetz], and Nakło with all the cities in its vicinity. They were annexed by Poland, which meant that Bolesław now ruled the access routes to the sea through the Noteć swamps and, in effect, sealed the fate of the Vistula basin of Pomerania.

Information regarding the second part of Bolesław Krzy-wousty's reign presents a problem, because the entries of the very faithful chronicler Gall Anonim stop in the year 1113. The sequence of events which followed are recorded in fragments with many lacunae and points that are difficult to explain.

The period between 1113 and 1123 saw a bitter struggle for control of Pomerania. The Polish attack was directed against the eastern part and the sole account of these wars gives only a single detail: that two cities were taken in the year 1116. This probably occurred during the final phase of the annexation of the Vistula basin of Pomerania, because entries for the year 1119 already pertain to battles in the western part of Pomerania. At the conclusion of the campaign in Eastern Pomerania, a revolt broke out in 1117 led by the wojewoda Skarbimir, who had been Bolesław's precep-tor and now declared his opposition to him. The reason for the rebellion is unknown, as is what inclined Krzywousty's old friend and guardian to take part. Perhaps it was related to the struggle of the magnates against the growing power of the prince. The revolt was bloodily suppressed, and despite all his previous services Skarbimir was blinded as a traitor.

Bolesław had no intention of desisting after regaining Eastern Pomerania, rather proceeding with a plan to occupy the long-independent territories along the lower Oder and Parsenta [Per-sante]. The war in these areas was all the more difficult because the pagan Pomeranians not only were fighting for their political freedom, but were fiercely opposed to any attempts to christianize them. In the course of several campaigns between 1119 and 1123, even the most fortified centers fell. Szczecin [Stettin] was taken in the winter, when deep freezes permitted access to the city along its surrounding waterways. Bolesław also finally took the islands of Uznam [Usedom] and Wolin.

That was the order of events in the conquest of Pomerania, but Bolesław treated the occupied territories in various ways. The area along the Noteć was annexed in its entirety to Wielkopolska and Polish governors ruled in the area of the Vistula basin of Pomerania, though they had been recruited from local dynasties, but Western Pomerania continued to be ruled by its reigning prince, Warcisław, who acknowledged Polish suzerainty. He was obligated to provide military troops for Bolesław's campaigns, pay an annual tribute, and convert to Christianity.

Krzywousty placed special emphasis on this last condition because he realized that church ties between a converted Pomerania and the Gniezno metropolitan would strengthen the bonds between the two states. The missionary effort faced serious problems, however, because of a lack of priests within the Polish episcopate capable of undertaking such a project. Bolesław was compelled to seek help elsewhere. Bishop Bernard, a Spaniard by descent, accepted the mission, but it failed primarily because of a lack of understanding of the pagan Pomeranians' nature and customs. In order to find another candidate, Bolesław turned to Otto, the bishop of Bamberg, who knew Poland from several journeys he had taken there and who had an advantage over Bernard because he spoke the local language. Otto accepted the mission and, after receiving papal permission, arrived in Poland in 1124.

Bolesław paid all of the costs of the mission. He also placed all the missionaries under his protection, which later proved to be important when the pagan Pomeranians began to manifest their opposition. Otto remained in the north for almost a year and accomplished his task. When he returned in the spring of 1125, Otto came to Gniezno to discuss with Bolesław the future organ-

ization of the church in these territories. It was decided then that
the candidate for bishop of Pomerania was to be Wojciech, who
had accompanied Otto and had been Bolesław's chaplain.

The pagan elements were not easily extirpated. In 1127 an anti-
Polish revolt broke out in Western Pomerania, as well as a pagan
reversion in Szczecin and Wolin which so seriously damaged the
fragile Christian base that in 1128 an appeal was again sent to Otto
of Bamberg. On this occasion Warcisław himself, after realizing
the political consequences that church organization brought with
it, undertook to gain some measure of independence from Polish
influence by entering into secret and direct negotiations with
Otto. After consulting the German king, Otto responded to
Warcisław's appeal. This time Otto left for Pomerania as a representative, not of Polish interests, but of the empire's, whose interests in its eastern affairs had revived when Lothar of Supplinburg
came to the throne.

In these circumstances Warcisław desired to avoid any open
conflict with Bolesław, who had every intention of defending his
interest militarily, and he persuaded Otto to act as a mediary.
Warcisław not only again agreed to recognize Piast suzerainty, but
by a symbolic oblation in the Gniezno cathedral he also acknowledged the subordinate position of the Pomeranian church in
respect to the Polish metropolitan. Certain international as well as
local problems made it impossible to create a Pomeranian bishopric for the time being. The sources of the problem were, first,
the ambition of the bishop of Magdeburg to place all the northern
Slavic territories under his jurisdiction and, second, the particular
interests of Pomerania, which resisted all efforts to increase its
dependence on Poland.

These difficulties pertained only to Western Pomerania. The
situation in the eastern part was quite different. The western area
along the Noteć that had been annexed to Wielkopolska became
part of the diocese of Poznań, while the eastern part was joined to
the diocese of Gniezno, and the area of Pomerania along the Vistula, together with Kujavia, formed the newly created diocese of
Kujavia. Bolesław attempted to resolve questions regarding
church matters in Western Pomerania in a similar manner. The

proof lies in the creation of the small new diocese of Lubusz, which was carved from much older western dioceses. According to Bolesław's design, in time the new diocese was to expand its jurisdiction to the north and include Western Pomerania, while yet remaining subordinate to the Polish metropolitan.

Warcisław could not reconcile himself to Pomerania's loss of suzerainty. Once more during Bolesław's reign he attempted to break free from Polish dominance, confident that Pomerania's geographical position, sheltered by small flooding rivers and swamps, would facilitate a defense. Krzywousty turned to the Danes for aid, and during the campaign of 1129 (or perhaps 1130), he was able to seize Uznam and Wolin and once again force Warcisław to submit.

The course of Bolesław's Pomeranian policy was seriously hampered toward the end of his reign. In 1131 Krzywousty's Danish ally was at war with the empire and was forced to submit after being soundly beaten. In the same year another of Bolesław's allies, István II of Hungary, Kálmán's successor, died. This created a dangerous situation for Poland, because the new Hungarian king, Béla II, the son of Álmos who had been supported by the empire, was related to the prince of Bohemia and remained on good terms with the empire. Bolesław was apprehensive that Hungary would side with the German-Czech camp and, therefore, together with Rus he supported Béla's rival, Boris.

A Polish campaign undertaken in 1132 was a total failure. The troops sent by the Babenbergs joined the enemy, and Boris's supporters proved to be especially weak. Bolesław was unable to withstand the opposition alone and suffered a serious defeat. The Czechs began diversionary attacks against Silesia, ravaging the province in a series of four incursions (1132, 1133, and two in 1134).

Poland faced still another threat at the same time. Pope Innocent II finally submitted to the pressures applied by Emperor Lothar and Archbhishop Norbert of Magdeburg, and in 1133 he issued two bulls denying independence to the metropolitans of Gniezno and Lund. The Polish bishoprics were to be subordinate to Magdeburg, and the Scandinavian bishoprics were to be subject to Bremen. This decision, which opened the way for German influence to the north and the east, was a serious threat to Denmark's and Poland's independence. The episcopates of both countries were reluctant to submit to this papal order. They responded slowly and even attempted countermeasures by appealing to the antipope, Anacletus II.

At the most critical moment, when the independence of the Polish church hung in the balance and defeated Denmark had submitted to the emperor, Krzywousty was called before the emperor's court by Soběslav of Bohemia and Béla of Hungary. Finding himself in such an unfavorable political position that he could not depend on any support, Bolesław decided to check his opponents by arranging a compromise with the emperor. In spring 1135, Bolesław sent emissaries and gifts to the emperor and in August personally left for Merseburg. Obviously the emperor did not fail to exploit Bolesław's difficult situation, and he did not limit himself to matters pertaining to Bohemia and Hungary; rather, he demanded a full explanation of Poland's relationship to the empire. Because of the circumstances, Bolesław had to make concessions in every matter. He recognized Béla's suzerainty in Hungary, agreed to a truce with Bohemia, and finally, according to the tradition dating back to Mieszko, agreed to pay homage as lord of Pomerania and Rugia [Rügen] and pay the tribute which had been in arrears for many years (from 1123, or the year when Western Pomerania was conquered) and amounted to six thousand pounds of silver. These were formidable concessions that Krzywousty was obliged to make, since they amounted to an acknowledgment of the supremacy of the empire in Western Pomerania. The compromise included a positive feature: Bolesław gained the right to expand toward Rugia and to maintain the independence of the Polish church, which had been challenged by the claims of the archbishop of Magdeburg.

Unfortunately, the Merseburg agreement, which could have served as a means of further expansion in Pomerania if skillfully exploited, was signed at the very end of Bolesław's reign. The severe stress on his health resulting from the enormous efforts he had made during his reign led to Krzywousty's death at the age of fifty-two on 27 October 1138.

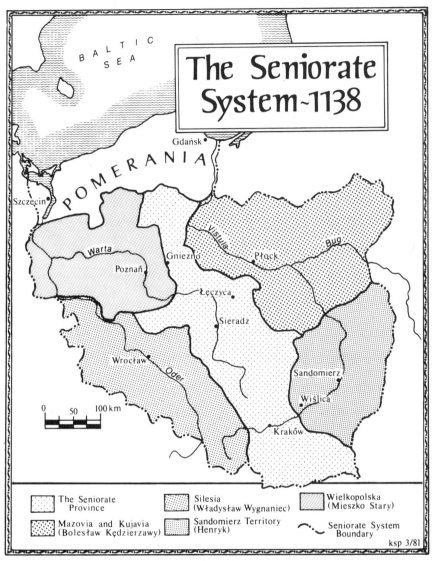

The Seniorate
System~1138

BALTIC
SEA

POMERANIA

Gdańsk

Szczecin

Warta

Poznań

Gniezno

Vistula

Płock

Bug

Łęczyca

Sieradz

Wrocław

Oder

Sandomierz

Wiślica

Kraków

0   50   100 km

The Seniorate Province	Silesia (Władysław Wygnaniec)	Wielkopolska (Mieszko Stary)
Mazovia and Kujavia (Bolesław Kędzierzawy)	Sandomierz Territory (Henryk)	Seniorate System Boundary

ksp 3/81

Map 5

Realizing that he would soon die, Bolesław desired to formalize a system of succession in order forever to preserve the country from civil war and to protect ducal rule from debilitating challenges by the magnates. Krzywousty therefore ordered that the honor of supreme prince, *princeps,* would fall to the oldest member of the dynasty, the "senior." He also declared that the princeps would receive, beyond his patrimony, a seniorate province composed of the Kraków, Sieradz, and Łęczyca districts, the eastern section of Wielkopolska, which included Kalisz and Gniezno, and the western section of Kujavia, including Kruszwica. This large province was intended to guarantee the princeps so preponderant an advantage that, at least theoretically, no one would dare to challenge him. Bolesław divided the remainder of the country among his four oldest sons, designating Silesia for Władysław, Mazovia and eastern Kujavia for Bolesław, Wielkopolska for Mieszko, and the Sandomierz and Lublin provinces for Henryk. [See map 5.] In contrast to the Russian system of succession, these provinces were to be hereditary in the respective branches of the dynasty; in the event that one of the lines should become extinct, the province would pass to the senior prince. The princeps also had suzerainty over Pomerania, the right to make administrative appointments in the major cities and invest bishops in the provinces of the junior princes, to collect court fines, to coin money, and, finally, supreme command over military affairs. Bolesław considered that if all members of the dynasty honored these statutes, then the unity of the state would be preserved and protected against upheavals which could come as a result of the intrigues of the magnates for free elections of a princeps.

Fate dictated otherwise. Krzywousty's testament, meant to preserve the state from internal upheaval and protect its unity, became the cause of numerous conflicts that eventually resulted in the collapse of the monarchy.

10

The Unstable
New Order

Krzywousty's two marriages produced numerous offspring. With his first wife, Zbysława, the daughter of the Kievan prince, Sviatopolk, Bolesław had one son, Władysław, who was born in 1105, and a daughter whose name is unknown and who was six years younger. With his second wife, Salomea, who was the daughter of the count of Berg, he had fourteen children, of whom ten survived. Of this number, four were sons: Bolesław Kędzierzawy [the Curly-haired], who was born in 1125; Mieszko, who was a year younger and later received the epithet "Stary" [the Old]; Henryk, who was born in 1127; and finally, Kazimierz, who was born the same year that Krzywousty died. Since Kazimierz was destined in all probablity for the religious life, he was not included in his father's last testament.

Of the five sons named above, Władysław and Bolesław had married before their father's death. Władysław's sons were already adolescents. His marriage was one of the most splendid in the history of the Piast dynasty. Władysław's wife, Agnieszka of the Babenbergs, the daughter of Leopold III of Austria, had family connections throughout the empire. Her brothers were Leopold IV of Austria; Henry (II) Jasomirgott; Otto, the bishop of Frisia; and Conrad, the archbishop of Salzburg; her sister Gertrude eventually married Vladislav, who became prince of Bohemia in 1140. But Agnieszka was especially proud of her half-brother, Conrad Hohenstaufen, who was elected king of Germany (7 March 1138) after Lothar's death. Neither Krzywousty's widow nor her oldest son, Bolesław Kędzierzawy, who had married Wierzchosława, the daughter of the prince of Novgorod, Vsevolod, could claim such splendid family ties. This fact very quickly became the source of a mutual animosity between these two ambitious princesses and weighed heavily on the future relationship between the princeps and his brothers.

Agnieszka was so vain regarding the status of her family that she considered her husband's position as princeps to be beneath her dignity. To paraphrase the Polish chronicler Kadłubek's words, she contemptuously called her husband a half-prince or half a man and incited him to exile his brothers. For the time being Władysław ignored his wife's abuse and demands. Not only did he allow his two oldest half-brothers to assume the lands to which they were entitled, but he also placed part of the seniorate province at the disposition of Krzywousty's widow for the remainder of her life and agreed to permit her to act as regent in the lands bequeathed to her young son, Henryk.

Władysław's rather compliant attitude could be explained by the role of the magnates, who desired to weaken the princely authority and saw they could realize their purpose by supporting the interests of the junior princes. The princeps did not have the means to confront such powerful opponents, and Władysław could not rely on aid from his brother-in-law, who was entangled in a civil war within the empire.

Conrad III, who was supported by the clergy and the nobility in the south of the empire, was opposed by Lothar's son-in-law, Henry the Proud, one of the most powerful German princes. Henry ruled Bavaria, which had been in the hands of the house of Welf for several generations, and he had expectations regarding Saxony. He was heir to the emperor's private estates and was also lord of Tuscany and Countess Matilda's heir. As a result of intrigues by the nobility, who were afraid of Henry's power, he was denied the imperial crown which he had so desired. He therefore wanted at least to secure control of Saxony, which he had been promised. The rise in power of such a rival was hardly in Conrad's interest, and, under the pretext that two principalities could not be ruled by a single prince, he denied Henry's petition and gave Saxony to one of the most devoted friends of the Hohenstaufens, Albert of Ballenstedt, who was commonly known by the epithet "the Bear." This imperial decision plunged the entire empire into civil war in the summer of 1138.

Despite the support Conrad III received from the clergy and the princes of the empire, he could not resolve the conflict. Nor did the situation improve when the principality of Bavaria was taken from Henry and given to the Babenbergs at the Diet of Goslar in December 1138. The rebellious prince, who had the support of the dowager empress, the archbishop of Magdeburg, and Conrad, the margrave of Meissen, crushed Albert the Bear in battle and forced him out of Saxony. This defeat placed Conrad III in so difficult a position that he did not dare confront Henry in battle, and in the summer of 1139 he requested a truce of several months.

Suddenly, the situation in the empire was drastically altered. Within several months, in October 1139, Henry the Proud died and left a widow and a young son, also named Henry, who would later receive the epithet "the Lion." But Conrad was unable to take advantage of this favorable turn of events, and Albert the Bear, who could not rely on Conrad's help, was again routed by the Saxon nobility, who recognized only the authority of the house of Welf. The rebellion spread to Bavaria, where the deceased Henry's brother successfully expelled the Babenbergs.

In these circumstances, Conrad had no choice but to seek some kind of compromise with his opposition. In May 1142, an agreement was concluded in which Henry the Lion received Saxony. In exchange Conrad was able to secure Bavaria for his half-brother, Henry Jasomirgott, who married Henry the Proud's widow. Albert the Bear was given the Nordmark.

This four-year period of unremittant civil war, which made it impossible for Conrad to intervene on behalf of his brother-in-law in Poland, was used to full advantage by Princess Salomea to consolidate the opposition against the princeps. In order to establish formidable dynastic ties, she arranged a marriage between her second son, Mieszko, and Elżbieta, the sister of the Hungarian king, Béla II. She then attempted to renew old bonds with members of German families who had been close to her own family. A measure of Salomea's success was the marriage of her daughter,

Dobronega Ludgarda, to Dietrich, the son of the influential margrave of Meissen, Conrad. Finally, in order to gain another ally in the inevitable conflict with the princeps, Salomea proposed, at a council with her sons in Łęczyca in 1141, to give her three-year-old daughter Judyta in marriage to one of the sons of the new grand duke of Kiev, Vsevolod.

It is difficult to believe that all of Salomea's maneuverings escaped Władysław's attention, but the mere fact that he had not been invited to the council in Łęczyca should have signaled the nature of his stepmother's actions and made him more cautious. At least he was able to circumvent Salomea in the Kievan matter by arranging a marriage between his own son, Bolesław, and one of Vsevolod's daughters.

This diplomatic success certainly determined Władysław's further course of action. Since he could rely on Russian reinforcements, in 1142 Władysław attacked his brothers and occupied several major cities, although a record of the names of the cities has not been preserved. The princeps's action alarmed the magnates, who desired least of all to see his authority increase. Led by Archbishop Jakub ze Żnina and by Wszebor, the wojewoda from Krzywousty's reign, many of the magnates joined the camp of the junior princes, which gave them enough support to repel any of the princeps's attacks.

Because neither side had enough confidence in its strength to conduct a campaign to its conclusion, the conflict was left in abeyance until a more opportune time. The princeps made every effort to remain on good terms with the Russian princes; to reciprocate the aid Władysław had received, in 1144 he sent troops to Grand Duke Vsevolod for his campaign against the prince of Galicia, Volodimirko.

The death of Princess Salomea on 27 July 1144 occasioned new disagreements between the brothers. When Władysław attempted to repossess the lands he had granted to Salomea only for the remainder of her life, he was resisted by his brothers, who considered the land their rightful patrimony. With the support of the local magnates, they occupied Łęczyca.

Just as he had done two years earlier, Władysław requested aid from Kiev, and the junior princes intensified their efforts to form alliances with the magnates opposed to the princeps. Their diplomatic efforts were quite extensive. At the council which they called in Gniezno for 2 March 1145 in order to discuss preparations for the imminent Russian invasion, the papal legate Humbald also participated; he probably had instructions to resolve the disagreement between the brothers. When Władysław entered the disputed territory with his Russian reinforcements, they met considerable resistance. The armies confronted one another in the boggy area along the middle section of the Pilica River, where the weaker forces of the junior princes won a victory over the older brother. They were not able to pursue their advantage; perhaps the first battle took place before the arrival of the Kievan troops. In any case, the junior princes agreed to negotiate and concluded a peace that was barely favorable to their cause. In order to retain the northern section of Salomea's legacy, they surrendered four castles and the surrounding areas in their territories to Władysław. They ceded the Mazovian city of Wizna to Władysław's Russian allies. The peace was concluded with a ceremonious pledge according to a Russian ritual.

Despite the appearance of victory, this agreement amounted to a resounding defeat for Władysław. Not only did Władysław fail to usurp his brothers' provinces, but he even failed to regain a significant part of the territory which was rightfully his and that he had granted to Salomea only for her lifetime. He entered into negotiations with the junior princes and was compelled to disclaim his supremacy over them, recognizing them as suzerain princes in the presence of his Russian allies. In fact, this was not only a victory for the junior princes, who had emancipated themselves from the power of the princeps, but also a victory for the secular and clerical members of the magnate class, who were more than content to see the power of the Krakovian princeps weaken.

Władysław fully realized the seriousness of his situation, and though he had not given up the idea of confronting his brothers in the future, he decided that for the present he must first dispose of the magnates who supported them. His inborn lack of tact and restraint only worsened the situation. Because he suspected Piotr Włostowic, who had been his devoted ally, of clandestinely ac-

commodating the junior princes, he decided to punish him severely. Making an example of Piotr Włostowic was a risk that
was entirely out of proportion. Piotr Włostowic was one of the
most powerful Polish magnates, having extensive family ties and
numerous clients, especially in Silesia. His personal wealth was
legendary, and the generosity with which he endowed the numerous churches and monasteries he had built contributed to his
reputation abroad, which held that he was a sovereign prince. He
had been elevated by Krzywousty to the position of wojewoda
and proved himself an able leader when, in order to protect his
king from an attack by Volodar of Przemyśl, he abducted this
Russian prince and forced him to abandon his invasion plan. After
Krzywousty's death, Piotr Włostowic was one of Władysław's
most faithful allies and friends. If Władysław could choose such a
man as the object of his revenge, then there must have been
further considerations. Perhaps there is a certain element of truth
in the legend which surrounds his fall concerning a personal disagreement between Piotr Włostowic and Władysław's vengeful
wife, Agnieszka. In any case, he was punished as a traitor, placed
under house arrest toward the end of 1145, and then, on
Władysław's orders, blinded and sentenced to exile.

The extremity of the punishment was meant to remind the
magnates of Krzywousty's pattern of strong rule and the punishment he had meted out to the once devoted Skarbimir, but the
effect was precisely the reverse of what Władysław had anticipated. The injustice committed against Piotr Włostowic not only
left Władysław without the support of Piotr Włostowic's numerous relatives and clients, but also antagonized the remainder of the
magnates who had previously given him their support.

The situation grew more tense, and within several months
open conflict broke out between Władysław and his half-brothers.
On this occasion Władysław not only requested Russian troops,
but also turned to the pagan Prussians and Jadzwings for aid.
They launched an attack from three directions in the beginning of
1146 which completely confused the armies of the junior princes.
Their defeated remnants hurriedly retreated to Wielkopolska,
leaving the rest of the Polish territories in Władysław's hands.

Władysław was confident that he was at the height of his success and complete victory was not far off. He merely had to take Poznań, to which the young princes had fled with the remnants of their armies, and this appeared to be a very simple task. But his expectations were not to be realized. As Poznań was stubbornly resisting the siege, a rebellion broke out in the lands which Władysław had occupied. The venerable Archbishop Jakub, who was frustrated by his inability to reconcile the feuding princes, placed Władysław under anathema as an enemy of peace and an ally of paganism. Władysław ignored all these signs of trouble, and during the siege of Poznań he did not even maintain elementary caution. The besieged princes were able to contact the leaders of the rebellion and to plan a two-sided simultaneous attack against Władysław. The element of surprise was complete, and Władysław's army was routed. Władysław himself did manage to escape to Kraków. Because his campaign had failed, Władysław's foreign allies abandoned him, and his domestic allies were also leaving his ranks. This forced him to turn to the empire for aid. His wife and children remained in Kraków while Władysław hurried to Conrad's court by way of Bohemia, arriving in Saxony by Easter Sunday, 31 March 1146. He took the oath of a vassal before his brother-in-law in exchange for a promise of intervention. Meanwhile, the troops of the junior princes were at the walls of Wawel Castle in Kraków. The city attempted to defend itself, but it was not prepared to withstand a prolonged siege and was forced to capitulate. The victorious junior princes did not imprison Agnieszka, but allowed her to take her children and follow Władysław into exile.

In spite of certain personal concerns and domestic disturbances in the south of the empire, Conrad decided to intervene on Władysław's behalf and set out to the east with a relatively small army in August 1146. This hardly came as a surprise to Władysław's brothers, who in anticipation of this campaign had fortified a defensive line along the Oder. The poorly planned German expedition was prevented from passing this first obstacle, and Conrad decided to negotiate in order to salvage part of his already compromised authority. The intermediaries who arranged an

agreement between the two sides were members of the Saxon nobility, with Albert the Bear and Conrad of Meissen at the head of
the delegation. With their aid, a settlement was quickly concluded
by which Conrad agreed that, in return for a monetary settlement
and a promise by all parties to appear before the imperial court, he
would recognize the existing state of affairs in Poland and refrain—
at least for the time being—from any attempt forcefully to restore
Władysław to power. At the conclusion of the negotiations the
imperial army withdrew from Silesia, and the unfortunate exile,
Władysław, together with his family, settled in Saxony at the castle
of Altenburg, which his brother-in-law had placed at his disposal.
Władysław accepted one more defeat after the unsuccessful imperial
intervention: in order to place another obstacle in the path of
Władysław's return, his brothers had appealed to the Curia to up-
hold the anathema placed on Władysław by Archbishop Jakub during the siege of Poznań, and it was confirmed.

The powers of the princeps were assumed by Bolesław Kędzierzawy, who divided part of Władysław's lands among his
brothers, Mieszko and Henryk. The brothers were not anxious to
fulfill the conditions of the peace agreement, and Conrad was too
occupied by other matters to consider their behavior a new cause
for war.

The entire West was feverishly preparing for a new crusade,
which Saint Bernard persuaded Conrad to join also. There could
be no thought of a new campaign against Poland for the present,
and only diplomatic measures were taken. The most serious impediment still weighing heavily on Władysław was the papal anathema. It was an obstacle to every attempt at reaching an understanding with the Apostolic See. In order to remove this burden,
Conrad took measures to have the anathema against Władysław
rescinded. Władysław probably participated in the campaign to
the Holy Land in order to atone for his guilt. By this act of
expiation he intended to regain the favor of the Apostolic See and
open a path for his return to Poland.

The fever of the crusades did not fail to infect Poland. The
young princes desired to preserve the goodwill of the Saxon nobility, which was most important because Saxony was the resi-

dence of their exiled brother. They decided that instead of joining the crusade to the Holy Land they would take part in a campaign against the Polabian Slavs. This crusade was not really in Poland's interests, but it brought one advantage. An alliance was signed with Albert the Bear in Kruszwica on 6 January 1148. A marriage also was arranged between Albert's son, Otto, and Judyta, the sister of the Polish princes.

Agnieszka too was not merely biding her time. She took advantage of her personal influence in the imperial chancellery to request that the regency of Conrad's young son, Henry, who formally ruled in his absent father's place, send an official request to the pope to reconsider Władysław's case. The petition complemented the Curia's tendency to play a more significant role in relation to secular matters, and it was favorably received. Toward the end of 1148, the pope sent a special legate, Cardinal Guido, to study the Polish situation firsthand. Following the adamant instructions of the Curia, the cardinal categorically demanded the reinstatement of the exiled princeps. When his demands were met with an equally adamant refusal by the princes, he anathematized them and placed Poland under interdict. Now the cardinal was confronted by his first serious obstacle. The Polish clergy who supported the princes refused to comply with the legate's orders regarding both the anathema and the interdict.

In these circumstances, Guido had no choice but to leave the country and inform the Curia of the complications. The information was received indignantly in Rome, and the Curia demanded that Conrad, who had just returned from the Holy Land, mount a military campaign against these Polish princes who had ignored ecclesiastical authority. Difficulties within the empire, especially a new threat of civil war, left Władysław helpless in this final chance to regain his legacy.

The exile in Altenburg began to appear permanent, and Władysław started to form greater ties with the land where he had found sanctuary. He was often present at the emperor's court, and his heirs, as well as other cousins of the Hohenstaufens, became objects of their dynastic politics. For example, in 1151 Władysław and Agnieszka's daughter, Ryksa, was betrothed to Alfonse VII of

Castile, who also had the title of emperor of Spain. The brothers-in-law, Władysław and Conrad, remained on very good terms despite the long exile of this Piast in Altenburg and the lack of good fortune in his life.

Conrad's death on 15 February 1152 and Agnieszka's death, which soon followed, changed the situation for the worse. Frederick Barbarossa, Conrad's successor, had no ties whatsoever with the Polish exile and was entirely indifferent to his fate. If the new emperor were to turn his attention to Władysław's cause in the future, it would be only a pretext to renew a conflict over imperial rights in the east.

11

Poland's Retreat from Its Western Policies

German expansion toward the Slavic east had been neglected in the second half of the eleventh century, but it was revived when Lothar of Supplinburg came to power in Saxony, then becoming in turn both the German king and the Holy Roman Emperor. He was the one responsible for appointing those individuals to the provinces along the Polish border who left an indelible mark in the German drive toward the east. They were Albert, the count of Ballenstedt, known as "the Bear," who first ruled the Lusatian Mark and then the Nordmark, and who was the progenitor of the Ascanian dynasty, and Conrad, the margrave of Meissen, who was the founder of the Wettin dynasty.

Albert was especially energetic in his efforts to annex territory, because just two years after receiving the Nordmark (1134) he instigated a dispute with the ducal family of the Brzeżans, whose lands were on the east bank of the Elbe, and occupied the territory in 1136. This territory in turn became Albert's base for attack and expansion into Lutician territory. German pressure was applied both to the Lutician territories and to those lands inhabited by the Obodrites. They were then ruled by two princes: Przybysław, who controlled the western part, and Niklot, who ruled the eastern section. When Przybysław destroyed one of the Saxons' frontier settlements, his action became a pretext for a general invasion of his principality by Albert. The campaigns of 1138 and 1139 resulted in the annexation of this western Obodrite territory. A German count was appointed to the territory, who, in order to protect himself from a rebellion among the Obodrites, began to settle the annexed territory with German colonists from the west.

At the very time when the Germans became more aggressive in this area, a process of retreat from the lands conquered by Krzywousty had begun in Poland. Krzywousty's oldest son and heir to the administration of the state, Władysław, was consumed by plans to divest his half-brothers and failed to protect Polish interests in Pomerania. The papal bull of 1140 concerning the Pomeranian bishopric was silent on the subject of its dependence on the metropolitan of Gniezno, which further complicated the problem. If the political emancipation of Western Pomerania did not follow after it gained ecclesiastical independence from Poland, the reason probably was the young age of Warcisław's sons, Bogusław and Kazimierz, who succeeded him after he was assassinated in 1135.

The lack of initiative on the part of the Polish princes was also apparent in matters concerning the Prussians. The missionary effort undertaken in 1141 by the bishop of Olomouc [Olmütz], Zdík, was a failure due to a lack of support by Polish secular authorities.

As Poland became more passive, the German penetration into the Slavic territories broadened. This expansion was not always military. The neighboring Saxons were also adept at aggrandizing their position by peaceful means. The history of Brandenburg is a prime example: Albert the Bear supported and maintained friendly relations with Prince Przybysław of the Stodorans, a small Lutician tribe, and in 1142 he became Przybysław's heir to Brandenburg over the claims of his relatives. Another example was the alliance formed in the same year among Conrad, the margrave of Meissen, and the Polish junior princes, which was sealed by the marriage of the margrave's son, Dietrich, and Dobronega.

The Saxon noblity was even able to continue its plan of expansion under the aegis of a crusade declared by the Apostolic See. They proposed that, instead of joining the campaign against the Saracens, they would undertake a crusade against the nearby pagan Slavs, thereby not only fighting for the church but also furthering the private ambitions of German expansion. This proposal was accepted by the main propagator of the crusade, Saint Bernard, and confirmed by the Apostolic See. The participants in the crusade against the Slavs were granted indulgences which had previously been granted only to the crusaders in the Holy Land.

The Czechs, Danes, Frisians, and even the English offered the Saxons their aid. The Polish princes also participated. They were blinded by fear of the return of their exiled brother and joined the crusade in order to demonstrate their allegiance to the Saxon lords, despite the fact that their support of German expansion into Slavic territory was contrary to the cardinal principles and interests of the Polish state. Mieszko Stary commanded the Polish troops, while his older brother, Bolesław Kędzierzawy, took advantage of church indulgences offered to the crusaders by organizing a campaign against the Prussians.

The armies of the crusaders gathered at Magdeburg on the feast day of Saints Peter and Paul on 29 June 1147. They decided to concentrate their attack against the Obodrites and Luticians, while the assembled fleet of Danish, Frisian, and English ships would aid them from the sea. For three months the lands of the Polabian Slavs were ravaged and deep incursions into already Christianized areas of Pomerania followed. Despite the fact that such force had been applied, the results were minimal, and the crusaders were compelled to arrange a truce and return home by autumn.

But the crusade had a particular epilogue in terms of Polish-Saxon relations, and an agreement was reached the following January in Kruszwica. Both parties were eager to negotiate. Albert the Bear desired a guarantee that if his rival to the throne of Brandenburg, Jaksa, now living in Poland, raised a challenge regarding the principality of the Stodorans, he would not be granted Polish aid. The Polish junior princes wanted to negate their exiled brother's influence in the empire by forming a powerful counter-alliance. The negotiations did result in an agreement.

The terms of the alliance had to be applied shortly thereafter. When the prince of the Stodorans, Przybysław, died in 1150, Albert the Bear occupied Brandenburg because his rival, Jaksa, could not contest the margrave's military superiority. Jaksa was resigned to wait for an opportune moment, and this came toward the end of 1154, when Albert the Bear accompanied the emperor on one of his many Italian campaigns. Jaksa then rallied all of his allies and relatives, of whom he had many in Poland thanks largely to his marriage to Piotr Włostowic's daughter. He marched to the land of the Stodorans and took Brandenburg without difficulty. Before Albert was able to return to the area of the Elbe, Jaksa fortified his position there to the point that Albert was not able to displace him by relying on his own army. Albert was now compelled to bide his time and wait for an opportunity to retaliate.

Marian Gumowski ties the events in Brandenburg to the German campaign against Poland in 1157. He considers that Albert accused the junior princes of aiding Jaksa and that, after joining Władysław's supporters, he inclined the emperor to restore Władysław to power. Since this demand for redress alone would not be enough to convince the emperor, Albert preferred an opportunity which could prompt Frederick to act—namely, to restore all the powers of suzerainty over Poland which the empire had once enjoyed. Albert's efforts were supported by Vladislav of Bohemia, and together they obtained the emperor's permission to prepare a campaign against Poland. The general campaign was preceded by Albert's attack on Brandenburg.

The German preparations were known to the Polish princes. When in April 1157 Albert's army stood outside the walls of Brandenburg, the junior princes were thinking only of how to defend themselves, and they left Jaksa to his fate. After a stubborn defense, Jaksa realized that he could not continue to resist and entered into negotiations with Albert. The compromise decision was to divide the principality of the Stodorans between the two rivals; Albert then received the area of Brandenburg in the west, while Jaksa took Kopanica (today known as Köpenick, a district of Berlin) in the east.

Abandoning the principality of Brandenburg to its own fate did not save Poland from invasion. After the emperor had sent an ultimatum to the junior princes in Poland, the content of which is unknown, he crossed into Silesia in August 1157. The Saxon nobility and Czech troops under Vladislav's command accompanied him. The Polish princes had obtained mistaken information from their German informants and did not prepare an adequate line of defense along the Oder. The Germans crossed near Głogów and quickly moved east. Bolesław Kędzierzawy's tactics of destroying settlements and retreating deep into the country were a total failure. Alarmed by the rapid advance of Frederick's army, Bolesław appealed to Vladislav of Bohemia to act as an intermediary and signed a truce with the emperor. The terms were in large measure humiliating.

Bolesław remained the recognized ruler of Poland over the violated rights of his exiled brother, but he was forced to go to Frederick's camp in Krzyszków and pay homage to him, promising to obey the emperor's decision regarding the claims of the exiled Władysław, to participate in the emperor's Italian campaign, and to pay a penalty for procrastinating in fulfilling the obligations of a vassal. After his success, the emperor did not continue to pursue Władysław's cause beyond obtaining a promise that his patrimonial province, Silesia, would be returned to him. Gumowski feels that Albert the Bear advised the emperor to take this course after he had regained Brandenburg. Albert did insist that the junior princes fulfill the points of the agreement at Kruszwica and abandoned his support of Władysław's claims. The guarantee that the junior princes would comply loyally with the conditions of the treaty was the German insistence on hostages, with the youngest Piast, Kazimierz, included among them.

Bolesław Kędzierzawy did not intend to honor these humiliating conditions. He did not send the troops he had promised for the emperor's Italian campaign, and, taking advantage of the emperor's involvement in a distant war, he did not return Silesia to Władysław. Only after Władysław's death and the threat of a new intervention (and perhaps because he desired to have the hostages returned) did Bolesław decide in 1163 to restore Silesia to Władysław's sons, who in any case could not have pretensions to the power of the senior prince because of their ages. When Bolesław gave his nephews their father's patrimony, he made it clear that it was a gift of his personal generosity and demanded that they renounce all hereditary rights to Silesia. Bolesław further retained control over several of the more important cities, but when Władysław's sons finally consolidated their position in the lands which had been restored to them, they declared that the oaths they had taken were made under duress and were void. A struggle began with the senior prince after his garrisons in the major Silesian cities were forced to evacuate.

Another civil war ensued, with neither side gaining the advantage until 1172, when Bolesław finally defeated his nephews and forced them out of Silesia. They appealed to the emperor for protection, who threatened Bolesław with military intervention. Bolesław well remembered his lack of success in 1157, and without further resistance he paid a large tribute and returned Silesia to his nephews (1173). The emperor's role had enormous significance in that Władysław's sons agreed to pay a permanent tribute to the emperor for his intercession, which further increased their dependence on the empire.

During the war with the princeps, both of Władysław's older sons, Bolesław Wysoki ["the Tall"] and Mieszko Plątonogi ["Stumblefoot"], solidly supported one another and had no intention of dividing their patrimony. This state of affairs changed when the situation in Silesia had been resolved. Władysław's sons entered the orbit of their uncles' disputes regarding who would rule Kraków.

While the empire's influence increased along the Oder, Henry the Lion, the great antagonist of the Hohenstaufens, was making new gains along the Baltic. In 1160, the prince of the Obodrites, Niklot, was attacked and killed by the Saxons and their Danish allies. His sons did not surrender, continuing to resist with the aid of the Pomeranian princes, Bogusław and Kazimierz. They exploited the rivalries between Henry the Lion and Albert the Bear on the one hand, and between the Saxons and the Danes on the other. Then, in 1164, they called for a general revolt in the already subjugated territory of the Obodrites. In the struggle that followed, Henry the Lion won the final victory and the defeated Obodrites were forced to capitulate. Henry the Lion now quickly began to colonize these lands with villagers brought from overpopulated Flanders.

Two years later, in 1166, when the empire again was gripped by civil war involving the Hohenstaufens and Welfs, Henry the Lion became concerned that his enemies might provoke another Slav rebellion. Therefore, in 1167 he reached an agreement with

Niklot's son, Przybysław, whereby Henry returned all the lands of the Obodrites to Przybysław in exchange for his oath as a vassal. From that point on, this ancient Slavic dynasty became a faithful German servant, which permitted the Germans to gain complete control of these lands through entirely peaceful means. While the Obodrites succumbed to German expansion, the Danes systematically attacked the island of Rugia, until they finally forced the collapse of the rule of the Ranians there in 1168.

This wave of eastward German expansion also began to threaten the west Pomeranian princes. Bogusław of Szczecin could not find adequate support in the weakened and fragmented Polish state and became Henry the Lion's vassal in 1177. After Henry's fall he was included among the princes of the empire (1181).

The passage of only thirty years separated Krzywousty's death from the time when Poland's aspirations toward expansion were exhausted. Its borders in the west followed an ethnographic line and provided the Saxons with a base from which they could continue their incursion into Slavic territory.

12

The Abolition of Krzywousty's Testament

If Bolesław Kędzierzawy's efforts to overcome the claims of his exiled brother are omitted from the history of his reign, then the record of his long rule turns extraordinarily pale. Bolesław's only effort at extending his sphere of influence was in the Prussian territory neighboring Mazovia, but even these campaigns were not expansionist, but rather were preventive measures to protect Mazovia from Prussian raids. This defensive strategy brought minimal results because of operational difficulties in the wilderness of the border area. The number and extent of Prussian raids constantly increased, while Bolesław's countermeasures usually ended in disaster. The campaign which Bolesław organized in 1166 was a complete fiasco. Although Wincenty Kadłubek does not confirm it in his precise account of the campaign, Henryk, the prince of Sandomierz, was killed, together with many Polish knights.

Henryk had not married, and he named his youngest brother, Kazimierz, heir to all of his estates. Sandomierz was excluded from the legacy because Kazimierz's two older brothers contested the inheritance after Henryk's death. Kazimierz received only a small part of this territory—the region of Wiślica. Roman Grodecki noted that the creation of such a miniature principality really inaugurated the process of fragmenting the Polish state.

The magnates attempted to exploit this clear injustice against Kazimierz, but when they proposed the throne at Kraków to Kazimierz their real interest was to overthrow Bolesław. Negotiations conducted at a diet in Milica in 1172 regarding this matter had no result, because Kazimierz recognized the danger of confronting both of his older brothers and rejected the magnates' proposal. This decision prevented the organizers of the conspiracy from continuing their preparations for a coup. But the magnates did not wait long to see a change in authority at the capital in Kraków, because Bolesław Kędzierzawy died on 3 April 1173. In his testament Bolesław appointed Kazimierz guardian of his only son, Leszek, and regent over his son's lands. It is highly probable that Kazimierz was then able to reunite the whole Sandomierz territory under his authority.

Mieszko now became the princeps. He was politically prudent, mature, and a fervent defender of ducal power. He was a provident administrator who attempted to restore and increase the state treasury and tolerated few obstacles in the path toward his goal. But the fraud committed by his officials is legendary, and the falsification and tampering with the state's coinage by Mieszko's minters led to the impoverishment of many magnate families.

Mieszko married twice. His first wife was Elżbieta, the daughter of a Hungarian prince, Álmos, and his second wife was Eudoksia, the daughter of the grand duke of Kiev, Iziaslav. They provided him with eleven children: five sons and six daughters. This permitted Mieszko to arrange dynastic marriages on a grand scale. As a result, he drew numerous allies to his side from neighboring and distant states. He gave his daughters in marriage to Bernard, the son of Albert the Bear and future prince of Saxony; to Soběslav II, the prince of Bohemia; to Bogusław, a Pomeranian prince; to Bogusław's uncle, Racibor; to the ruler of the Vistulan basin of Pomerania, Mszczuj I; and to the prince of Lotharingia, Frederick. His sons married the daughters of Jaroslav Osmomysl ["the Eight-sensed"], prince of Galicia; of Warcisław, a Pomeranian prince; and of Jaromar, the prince of Rugia. These ties, some of which had been arranged before Mieszko had become princeps, increased his political power and allowed him to contemplate the restoration of the previous power and grandeur of ducal rule in Poland. Once Mieszko assumed power in Kraków, he began to appoint his devoted followers from Wielkopolska to state offices and relied on their continued support to consolidate his rule, particularly in the seniorate province.

These matters distressed the local magnate class, who had come

to value the independence they had achieved during the reign of
Bolesław Kędzierzawy. They had no intention of abandoning
their gains without a struggle. Under the leadership of Gedka, the
bishop of Kraków, the magnates turned to Kazimierz with a proposal that he rule in Kraków. Once they obtained his consent, the
conspiracy began to take form in earnest.

Kazimierz gave the signal for the revolt to begin when he entered the district of Kraków. He was enthusiastically welcomed
by the local population and did not encounter any significant opposition. Kraków was taken when the garrison opened the city
gates to him. This coup caught Mieszko completely by surprise,
especially the fact that his oldest son, Odon, had joined the conspirators and had taken up arms against his father in Wielkopolska. This act led many of Mieszko's supporters to abandon his
cause as well. Mieszko was forced to acknowledge that any defense was hopeless and, together with his three sons from his
second marriage, he fled to Pomerania. Mieszko's lands passed to
the victors and were divided by Kazimierz between Odon, who
received the principality of Poznań, and Leszek, who received all
of Kujavia. The remainder of Wielkopolska, together with Gniezno, remained within the borders of the seniorate province.

There were also repercussions in Silesia as a result of Mieszko's
overthrow: Mieszko Plątonogi, an ally of Mieszko Stary, rose up
against Bolesław Wysoki, who had sided with Kazimierz.
Plątonogi gained the support of the Silesian magnates and successfully overthrew his brother. This forced Kazimierz to intervene
on behalf of his ally, and he finally succeeded in restoring
Bolesław's lands to him. In order to preserve the peace in Silesia
and remove the causes of the dispute which Mieszko Stary could
always exploit through intrigue, all the brothers had to be guaranteed their lands. Through Kazimierz's initiative, Mieszko
Plątonogi received Raciborz, Bytom, Oświęcim, Siewierz, and
Chrzanów, while Konrad, a half-brother who originally had been
destined for the clergy, received the Głogów district. In analyzing
these territorial divisions, Grodecki came to the conclusion that
the district granted to Mieszko Plątonogi was carved almost in its
entirety from the Kraków-Sieradz-Łęczyca territory of the senior-

ate province. The reason for this curious decision was Kazimierz's desire not to diminish the territory of his Silesian ally, Bolesław Wysoki. He believed that once Mieszko Plątonogi had settled the lands that were joined by numerous economic and dynastic ties with Małopolska, he would certainly be pressed into demonstrating his allegiance to the princeps in Kraków.

The powers which Kazimierz assumed in Kraków derived from an act of usurpation, and, even after Mieszko Stary's exile, Kazimierz was not the senior member of the dynasty because Bolesław Wysoki was the eldest Piast. Predictably, one of Kazimierz's first concerns was to establish a legal right by which this usurpation could be legitimized. Kazimierz's good relations with the territorial princes facilitated his efforts, especially the fact that he recognized Bolesław Wysoki as the oldest representative of the Piast dynasty after Mieszko Stary. Kazimierz's position was finally acknowledged at a diet in Łęczyca in 1180. The entire episcopate of Poland, which had been specially invited by Kazimierz, joined the magnates at the diet. It was there that a resolution was approved to abolish the seniorate system and to transfer the Kraków territory to Kazimierz as a hereditary province. In order to gain the support of the nation's clergy, Kazimierz revoked his privilege of *ius spolii*—that is, to inherit the personal possessions of a deceased bishop. He also repealed the onerous laws pertaining to requisitions, which the magnates had freely exploited in relation to the peasantry. Kazimierz then turned to the Apostolic See for confirmation of the amended political structure. Because the Polish bishops were now his adamant supporters since the repeal of the *ius spolii,* Kazimierz obtained a bull of consent from Pope Alexander III. It recognized Kazimierz's rule in Kraków and declared the province hereditary in Kazimierz's line, which now replaced the Polish seniorate system.

These acts of legitimization regarding Kraków were opportune, because Mieszko Stary was exploiting his German connections and was desperately pleading for intervention at the imperial court. Despite his promise to pay the enormous sum of ten thousand silver marks, his efforts failed. Mieszko then managed to convince the Pomeranians to lend him their support. With their aid he made a sudden attack on Wielkopolska in 1181 and brought a large part of the province under his control, including Gniezno. Mieszko was able to regain these lands so easily because Kazimierz in fact did not oppose his brother's just claim to his inheritance. This concession did not assuage Mieszko's bitterness. On the contrary, he did all he could in order to subvert his brother's power and induce Kazimierz's allies to defect. Mieszko's intrigues led to a quarrel between Bolesław Wysoki and Kazimierz. Mieszko then took advantage of Bolesław's good relations with the Germans in order to advance his own cause at the imperial court. These efforts finally met with success. The emperor took enough serious interest in the matter to order his son, Henry VI, to undertake a campaign against Poland in August 1184.

Kazimierz was able to forestall the imminent threat for a time. He sent emissaries to Henry at Halle, and they conveyed the appropriate oaths of allegiance and inclined Henry to stop the campaign. The content of Kazimierz's message has not been preserved in the primary sources, but considering the results, Kazimierz must have recognized imperial suzerainty. Frederick's later relationship to Poland indicates that he treated Kazimierz as his vassal, which further supports this view.

Stanisław Smolka pointed to the fact that "many factors linked Kazimierz Sprawiedliwy with the Sandomierz territory, and because Sandomierz's most basic interests were tied to its relations with the neighboring Russian principalities, Kazimierz's policies were significantly affected by this relationship." Affairs in Russia left their imprint on Poland during this period and shifted political interests from a northwesterly direction to the southeast.

Kazimierz's interest in Russian affairs was all the more binding because of familial ties with the Riurik dynasty and their mutual conflict with Władysław Wygnaniec. While Władysław had entered into an alliance with Prince Oleg's sons, Krzywousty's younger sons relied on the support of Prince Mstislav's sons (a branch of the house of Monomakh). The junior princes had aided Mstislav's son, Iziaslav, in expelling Oleg's sons from Volynia. This relationship was further cemented through the marriage of Iziaslav's son, Mstislav, to the junior princes' sister, Agnieszka, in 1151 or 1152. The widowed Mieszko Stary then married Iziaslav's sister, Eudoksia. Kazimierz himself had been married to Iziaslav's niece, Halina, since 1163. [Recent scholarship indicates that Halina was probably Czech.]

After Mstislav's death in 1170, Volynia passed to his sons. Their cousin Vasilko, the son of Jaropolk, who was married to Bolesław Kędzierzawy's daughter, ruled in Drohiczyn. Kazimierz aided his nephews as well as Vasilko, whom he even helped to regain his proper inheritance. After Vasilko's death without an heir, Kazimierz was able to place the oldest of Mstislav's sons on the throne in Brześć. When a rebellion erupted in 1182 against this imposed prince, Kazimierz intervened militarily on his behalf. Kazimierz was forced to contend not only with the rebellion, but also with an open revolt by a large contingent of his own knights opposed to his Russian policies. Kazimierz was able to overcome the internal opposition and suppress the rebellion, after which he restored his nephew to power. When he was soon after poisoned by the conspirators in Brześć, Kazimierz transferred power in Volynia to the deceased prince's brother, Roman, who acknowledged Polish suzerainty.

When Kazimierz annexed Mazovia after Leszek's death in 1186, he took an even greater interest in Russian affairs. It was not confined to the lands ruled by his nephews. When the prince of Galicia, Jaroslav Osmomysl, died in 1187 and war broke out between his two sons, Oleg and Volodimir, Kazimierz supported Oleg. Volodimir was victorious and, in revenge for Kazimierz's support of his rival, invaded and ravaged a section of Polish territory. Kazimierz retaliated by entering into negotiations with Volodimir's Galician opposition; he placed Roman of Volynia on the throne, forcing Volodimir into exile in Hungary. The fact that Roman also now ruled in Galicia seemed to foreshadow that Polish suzerainty would be acknowledged there as it had been in Volynia. This was not to be, however, because Volodimir was able to involve the Hungarians in the dispute. The Hungarians had carefully observed events in Galicia with the intention of expanding beyond the natural border of the Carpathian Mountains. With Hungarian aid, Volodimir was restored, and Roman and Kazimierz were displaced from Galicia.

Hungary's intervention on Volodimir's behalf was obviously a convenient pretext to gain a foothold in Galicia. This became clear when the Hungarians realized how unpopular the restored prince was. They replaced him with King Béla III's son, András. He took the title "king of Galicia" (*rex Gallitiae*), which eventually passed to the kings of Hungary.

Volodimir was able to escape incarceration in Hungary and fled to the empire, where he appeared at the imperial court with a petition for aid in exchange for an annual tribute of two thousand marks. Frederick Barbarossa was occupied with preparations for the crusades and could not conduct a Russian campaign personally. He entrusted the task of restoring Volodimir to the throne of Galicia to his faithful vassal, Kazimierz Sprawiedliwy ["the Just"].

Kazimierz was compelled to abandon his own plans regarding Galicia, and in 1189 he entrusted the wojewoda, Mikołaj, with the campaign to restore Volodimir, the ruler whom he had previously overthrown. Kazimierz had jeopardized relations with Hungary with nothing to gain, since Volodimir would not acknowledge Polish suzerainty over Galicia. To make matters worse, Kazimierz also had lost suzerainty over Volynia when Roman abdicated in favor of his brother in order to rule in Galicia with Polish support.

These failures culminated in a breach between Kazimierz's supporters and opponents over the issue of his policy toward Rus and Hungary. The personal antagonisms among the leaders of both camps, and particularly the contempt they had for the devoted wojewoda, Mikołaj, led the opposition to set plans in motion for a coup. While Kazimierz remained in Rus with many of the knights who were still faithful to his cause, a conspiracy was organized by the castellan of Kraków, Henryk Kietlicz, who went to Mieszko Stary to offer him the Polish throne. The proposal was accepted and, with the support of the conspirators and an army from Wielkopolska, the stubbornly defended city of Kraków fell to Mieszko Stary in 1191.

Mieszko's success was short-lived. When Kazimierz learned of the coup, he immediately left for Kraków with Russian reinforcements. False rumors spread through the city that the Czechs were also sending reinforcements. This rumor had the effect of nullifying any resistance to Kazimierz's return, and he was able to retake the capital easily. Kazimierz won the allegiance of the conspirators through the magnanimity he displayed; he even released Mieszko's son without ransom after he had been captured. Kazimierz achieved an even greater reconciliation when he signed an agreement with the Hungarians a year later, in 1192. The agreement affirmed cooperative action in matters which affected both sides, such as the events that had transpired in Galicia. The negotiations with Hungary were conducted by Bishop Pełka of Kraków, and the wojewoda, Mikołaj, who had been attacked by the opposition for his earlier role in the entire affair.

In order to safeguard Mazovia, which had recently been victim to increased Jadzwing raids, Kazimierz undertook a retaliatory campaign against these pagan neighbors around 1193. Kazimierz first disposed of the Russian prince of Drohiczyn, who had assisted the Jadzwings. Kazimierz's armies then penetrated deep into the Jadzwings' territory, defeated them, and exacted an annual tribute to be paid to the prince in Kraków.

Soon after this victory, the fifty-six-year-old Kazimierz died suddenly during a banquet in 1194. The death of the prince generated a widely held opinion that his old enemies had poisoned him. Kazimierz's sudden death with his heirs still children portended serious complications for the state. His contemporaries realized the nature of these dangers. The chronicler Wincenty Kadłubek expressed his sorrow in a poem which reads: "When the lookout man leaves the prow of the ship, it crashes on the waves of the sea against the Syrtian sandbar and the hulls of wrecked ships. Then the storm that churns up from the deep blows the oars, loosened and lost, all over the sea."

13

The Political and Social Structure of Ducal Poland

The Piast dynasty's success in maintaining power was the principal reason for the collapse of the old order of clans, whose functions passed largely into the hands of the prince and his officials. In the circumstances which arose as a consequence of continuous wars, the prince necessarily had to assume the leadership of the social order, and his person was the force that unified the new political order.

Conversion to Christianity and the resulting broader ties with the West led Poland to adopt Western European laws and customs. This fact was particularly reflected in the organization of the state, which imitated the Carolingian model. The Frankish empire provided the model for many aspects of the political structure which developed in Poland during the eleventh and twelfth centuries.

In order to review this structure it is appropriate to begin with a description of the powers of the prince (*ius ducale*). This power became centralized and aggrandized, in contrast to the system during the period of tribal differentiation. The prince became lord of his country and all its people. He conducted foreign policy and could declare war and negotiate agreements at will. He was the source of laws and supreme judge. The prince also had the right of lay investiture and was the defender or chief advocate of the church. His power was limited only through the institution of the council (*wiec*), which was exclusively in the domain of the nobility and clergy in the Piast era. This relationship, however, typically was elastic during the Middle Ages. The function of the council depended on the prince. During the reigns of weaker princes, such as Władysław Herman, the council dominated, while the more forceful princes, such as Bolesław Krzywousty, ruled with virtual independence.

The relationship of the prince to the state was proprietary, as it was at that time in the West. The prince was considered the proprietor of the state as a whole and of all the lands which had not yet passed into private hands. He was the state's largest land-holder, possessing numerous estates and lands which had not yet been settled.

The state was regarded as a private demesne, which meant that proprietary rights were applied in matters of succession. After the death of the prince, all the male heirs convened to divide the personal estate as well as the entire principality. In order to pre-serve the totality of the state, it became customary for the reign-ing prince to select one of his heirs as his successor and princeps. The princeps was the sovereign ruler over the remaining members of the dynasty. He represented the unity of the state and his duty was to protect the state from fragmenting into independent pro-vinces. The nomination of a successor was the free choice of the prince, who could choose his youngest son and exclude the eldest. This freedom of action was revoked through Krzywousty's testa-ment (1138), which established the seniorate system. It was meant to safeguard the state from internecine wars and protect the prince's sovereignty from the threat posed by the magnate class. Circumstances proved Krzywousty's foresight to be myopic. The new order began to waver just eight years later, when the prin-ceps was exiled; the state then collapsed entirely after the Diet of Łęczyca in 1180, when the seniorate system was replaced by suc-cession by primogeniture in Kazimierz Sprawiedliwy's line.

The prince was the immediate lord and supreme judge over all the inhabitants of the state, which permitted him to require certain obligations to be fulfilled. These were called the "burdens" under ducal or Polish rule (*onera iuris ducalis sive iuris Polonici*). They were understood to include services (*servitia, angariae, perangariae*) performed for the prince and his officials as well as various pay-ments and tribute (*solutiones seu tributa*). The majority of these burdens are known through the privileges of immunity granted in the thirteenth century which repealed many of them. It could be assumed that they had been in effect for quite some time, but it would be difficult to date the precise span. Those services performed during times of war were of primary importance: personal service in the campaign (*wojna*); pursuing a defeated enemy within the borders of the state (*pogoń*); barricading roads and transit points of potential use to an enemy (*przesieka*); constructing or repairing fortresses and bridges; and garrison duties for protection of the fortress (*stróża*). An important aspect of the burdens was a guarantee of public safety, which meant that in the event of a crime, a public alarm was sounded (*krzyk*) and the criminal was pursued within the territory inhabited by the clan (*ślad*). There were also services regarding transport, such as providing draft animals to pull supply wagons (*powóz*) or the actual transfer of supplies (*przewóz, przewód*). A final category of rather laborious services pertained to the hunt.

Besides personal services and tributes, there was a special obligation which required that the prince or any of his officials be provided with quarters and temporary maintenance during their journeys. This burden was virtually ruinous for those who lived near communication routes that were frequently traveled.

Tribute was often paid in the form of farm animals, grain, and honey. The etymology of these tribute terms originates from these goods. The oldest tribute collected in farm animals was called *narzaz*, which was paid in swine. Oswald Balzer traces the etymology of this word to a cutting tool used to make notches to record the number of animals collected in tribute. It made a type of receipt. Various other farm animals in time were included in the tribute, such as cows and sheep. Tribute paid in grain was referred to as *poradlne* (from the word for plow) and *powołowe* (from the word for oxen, which were used in plowing). The tribute collected in honey always appeared under its Latin name, *urna mellis*.

Besides tribute, there were also various taxes collected for use of facilities maintained by the state. These were tolls collected for the use of bridges and certain roads on access routes to fairs and markets.

A major source of income for the ducal treasury was the so-called regalia, or the prince's guaranteed right to organize hunts and market fairs, to coin money, and to mine ores and fossiliferous materials.

The lack of a clear separation between the prince's private demesnes and those of the state was also evident within the treasury. Only a single treasury existed, from which funds were allotted for state expenditures as well as for the private accounts of the prince.

Poland's court was similar to the western model. It consisted of officials, court clerks, and numerous servants. There are no extant primary source materials providing a description of the court of the first Piasts, but because both the composition of the ducal court at the close of the twelfth century and that of the early Carolingian model on which the Piast court was based are known, it could be assumed with a high degree of probability that the Polish court in the eleventh century must have been similar to the original Carolingian court. In the beginning, the officials of the court had only one title, which was recorded only in its Latin form, *comites*. They were personal attendants to the prince and fulfilled various administrative functions. They were not appointed for specific terms, but were delegated authority according to need.

The highest official was the *palatyn* (*comes palatinus*). He was entrusted with supervision of the ducal court and was superior to all other officials and court attendants. The prince could empower the palatine to represent him in state affairs, in court matters, or in command of the army. When representing the prince as commander of a military force, the palatine later acquired the title *wojewoda*. In the event a succeeding prince had not yet come of age, or if a weak or incompetent ruler succeeded, the palatine assumed the role of the true ruler (as did Sieciech). The palatine's deputy was the *podkomorzy* (*subcamerarius*), who had the additional responsibility of managing the ducal estates. Even though in all probability the Piasts had not yet created a genuine chancellery, the office of *kanclerz* (*cancellarius*) did exist, and the *kanclerz* was the keeper of the ducal seal. This office was traditionally reserved for members of the church hierarchy. The prince's aide in matters of the courts was the *sędzia* (*iudex*), though he had no independent authority. Other officials and attendants included the *skarbnik* (*thesaurarius*), who administered the treasury; the *stolnik* (*dapifer*), who was charged with overseeing the royal table; the *czesnik* (*pincerna*), who cared for provisions and stores; the *miecznik* (*gladifer*), who preceded the king with sword in hand in ceremonies; and the *chorąży* (*vexillifer*), who was responsible for the ducal banners and standards. These officials were appointed by the prince and could be dismissed at will. They were granted land and provided with a state income.

The prince chose his immediate councillors from among the highest court dignitaries. According to Gall Anonim, the council was composed of twelve members.

The clergy played an increasingly important role. They were attached to the court chapel and, besides their pastoral functions, they aided the chancellor as copyists.

At the court there were also numerous minor officials, artisans, and servants of both sexes. All the servants were freemen.

The Piast princes frequently chose their brides from foreign courts, and the fact that they themselves remained outside the borders of Poland for extended periods contributed to an increasing foreign influence at court. Besides the foreign circle which surrounded the princess and the clergy, the prince recruited considerable numbers of foreign knights, which clearly gave the court a foreign and imported appearance.

The prince's authority, whether in domestic or foreign matters, was based on the military strength at his disposal. The Spanish Moor named al-Bekri (d. 1094) relates a description by Ibrahim ibn-Jakub, a Jewish slave merchant, who visited the court of Otto I in Merseburg in 973 and collected impressions of the empire and its neighbors. Ibrahim ibn-Jakub characterized Mieszko's retinue:

> He has three thousand knights and these are such warriors that ten thousand others could not equal a hundred of them. He provides them with garments, horses, weapons, and all that they require. When a child is born to any one of them, he contributes to its support, whether a boy or girl, and when the child matures, if it is male, he will arrange a marriage and provide the dowry to the father of the bride; if it is a girl, he also arranges a marriage and provides the dowry for her father.

It is logical to assume from the above that Mieszko's retinue represented the elite of his army. He depended upon it for his success in uniting the Lekhitic tribes and preserving the unity of his state. The proof of the existence of such a retinue among Mieszko's successors can also be documented.

Apart from the retinue, another class of knights gradually began to form from which the *szlachta* ["nobility"] would evolve. These knights represented the wealthier families of Poland as well as itinerant knights who had arrived in Poland to seek their fortunes. They were granted land by the prince, which afforded them the means to serve the prince militarily, and they further obtained various privileges which distinguished them with favored status. These privileges absolved them from certain obligations pertinent to the burdens under ducal law. The impact of these privileges generated a view that only knights could serve as official state administrators. In Gall Anonim's chronicle, there is an account of the nobility's alarm when the palatine Sieciech "elevated those of a lower class over those who were noble born" and entrusted them with state offices.

Particular knights were elevated above the rest, either because they were descended from past tribal dynasties or because they were the select beneficiaries of the early Piasts' endowments. These individuals, to whom great wealth had accrued, were called the *możni* ["magnates"]. They did not represent a distinct social class, but retained their ties with the knights from which they had evolved and to which they would return in the event they lost their wealth.

This division among the knights was the first stage of a further differentiation in the society. Those freemen who had not acquired enough wealth to place them in the category of knights were at the lower end of the new social hierarchy. A member of this group was called a *dziedzic* (*heres*). Poverty frequently forced members of this class to abandon their own lands and seek improved circumstances in other areas, where they cleared tracts of wilderness. They were then called *łazękowie*. The most impoverished of these *dziedzice* or *łazękowie* sometimes lost their independence by settling on property owned either by the church or by a knight. They did so either voluntarily, as *wolni goście* (*liberi hospites*), or as *przypisani* (*ascriptii*). This latter group lost its right to mobility and was no longer entirely free. Apart from the groups mentioned above, there was also a growing number of slaves and prisoners of war who were also bound to the soil in the rural population. They enjoyed a separate status and certain rights for a time, but those privileges were soon lost.

Ducal rule in the state was represented through the administration of the various *grody* (*castra*), or fortress settlements. The basis of this organization was the *gród* that had been in existence in the pre-Piast tribal period. Some of these settlements that were not necessary as defensive centers but could become points of support for a separatist movement were abandoned by the Piasts, which resulted in their complete decline. The remaining settlements were governed by an official *comes* of the prince, who would later come to be known as the *kasztelan*. His duties included insuring that the rural population strictly complied with their obligations to the prince and paid the required tribute. He also administered the prince's local estates through the office of the *włodarz*. Two of the most important duties of the *kasztelan* pertained to judicial matters involving small claims and command over the military force that could be recruited from the area under his jurisdiction.

Beyond the division of the state into *kasztelania*, there was a lesser administrative division into *opola* (*vicinia*). This was a grouping consisting of several to almost twenty neighboring settlements. The obligations of these *opola* were to provide proof before a court in matters of boundary disputes, pursue criminals within their boundaries (*ślad*), and deliver various kinds of tribute to the prince.

There were also larger districts consisting of several *kasztelania* and governed by a *namiestnik*. For example, Gall Anonim mentions the *comes* Magnus, who governed in Silesia in the eleventh century.

Mieszko organized his state on the Carolingian model and also began to mint a state coin based on Carolingian coinage. During the eleventh and particularly in the twelfth century, Piast coinage fell in value significantly; it contained less silver and the silver was of poorer quality. During the reign of Mieszko Stary, coins known as *brakteaty,* which were produced from very thin sheets of silver and stamped only on one side, were minted to meet a fiscal crisis and further contributed to the devaluation of Piast coinage. The fact that this coin was produced and issued three times a year further complicated the problem. Despite general protests, this method of coinage persisted until the fourteenth century. The Piasts did, however, permit the church to issue its own coins. Various coins were issued by mints established by the bishops of Poland during this period.

Trade routes leading from east to west and from south to north intersected Poland. The country contained active transit centers for merchants before its recorded history, and traveling merchants sold a portion of their merchandise while passing through Poland. The sale or bartering of goods was conducted in specified places where market fairs were established. They were located at central points along the trade routes, near cities, or in places where Christianity had already entrenched itself. These markets were under the protection of the *mir targowy,* a guarantee of safety for the merchants. These were also places where a modest internal trade began to develop and where various craftsmen began to settle. During the twelfth century, certain rights of free trade were granted to these areas to encourage commerce between the merchants and their clients. These rights were based on special judicial and financial privileges, as well as on a guarantee of safety to those who came to market, which was equivalent to the privileges enjoyed by members of the ducal court. This attracted numerous permanent settlers who took up residence outside the walls of a settlement, which in turn led to the growth of cities. Among these new settlers were a large number of foreigners.

Christianity had an enormous impact on the old customs of the nation and, under the pressure of the clergy, ancient customs that were contrary to the ways of the new religion were extirpated. Polygamy was prohibited, as was the custom of killing a widow at her husband's funeral. Other pagan beliefs and superstitions were also displaced. Where the church encountered its strongest opposition, it followed a practice of christianizing certain pagan customs. The church also imposed its own rituals and customs, which gradually began to penetrate more deeply into the lives of its converts. However, in Poland as well as in the West, the church was not able to mitigate the brutality of some customs, such as cutting out tongues or blinding accused traitors.

The church, however, was not the only civilizing influence. Many western customs were accepted by the ducal court through the influx of foreign knights. The presence of a substantial number of them resulted in the introduction of western manners at court. Gall Anonim provides proof of this in his description of the ceremony of young Bolesław Krzywousty's knighting.

The influence of the clergy and of the foreign arrivals at court generated an atmosphere which advanced education and literacy. Those who were destined for greater roles in the ecclesiastical hierarchy, in particular, pursued studies. It is highly probable that schools were established during this early period at some of the cathedrals in Poland for the purpose of educating students destined for the clergy. (Perhaps Zbigniew, Bolesław Krzywousty's brother, who was sent to Kraków for studies, attended such a school.) If Mieszko II's education was indicative of that of the early Piast princes, then it was quite adequate. Apart from the native language, the princes knew at least one other language, usually German or Russian, which they learned from childhood because their mothers were often of foreign origin. Latin also was not unknown to them, because it was both the language of the church and formally used in diplomacy. Mieszko II also knew Greek, which was a rarity in western Europe in that period.

Together with western manners and customs, various art forms filtered into Poland. Just as in the West, the arts were primarily in the domain of the church. The first stone churches in Poland were certainly erected with western skills, and the liturgical vessels and church decorations were made by western artisans and craftsmen. Very little has been preserved. Of the few precious works of the period which still remain, the bronze Drzwi Gnieźnieńskie, if they were created in Poland, furnish obvious evidence of masterful artistic craftsmanship in twelfth-century Poland.

appendixes

A
Glossary of Place Names

The Polish place names from the Manteuffel text appear in the first column of the table below. German equivalents are represented in column two, and the entries in column three are identified parenthetically according to language. The glossary of provinces contains the forms I have used in the text. The following abbreviations occur in the appendixes and introduction: (Cz) Czech; (E) English; (G) German; (L) Latin; (P) Polish; (R) Russian.

I have included both Czerwień and the Grody Czewieńskie in the appendixes. The references are to both a city and a territory which included some twenty or more cities and settlements located along the middle Bug and Wieprz rivers, with Czerwień at their core. The remaining cities in this territory are not identified in the primary sources. I have also used the form "Galicia," which may be interpreted as anachronistic, to refer to the twelfth-century principality located along the upper Dniester with the city of Halicz (P) at its center. The references to principal cities often implied a territorial sphere of influence. Past usage by Francis Dvornik, Michael Florinsky, Jesse Clarkson, and others indicates a high frequency of occurrence for Galicia (E) in references to the area, regardless of chronology. The principality of Volynia in the late twelfth century contained two major cities, Brześć and Włodzimierz [Vladimir-Volinsk (R)]. By the beginning of the thirteenth century, these two principalities were combined into one, called Księstwo Halickie (P), and again referred to as Galicia.

Cities

Białogród	Belgard	
Bełz	Belz	
Budziszyn	Bautzen	
Bytom	Beuthen	
Cedynia	Zehden	Cydzyna (L)
Czerwień		
Głogów	Glogau	
Gniezno	Gnesen	
Gradiec	Hradisch	Hradec (Cz)
Halicz	Galitsch	
Iomsborg	Jomsburg	
Kłodzko	Glatz	
Kołobrzeg	Kolberg	
Kraków	Krakau	
Krosno	Crossen	
Licykawa	Leitzkau	
Lubusz	Lebus	
Łęczyca	Lentschutz	
Międzyrzecz	Meseritz	
Nakło	Nakel	
Niemcza	Nimptsch	
Olomuniec	Olmütz	Olomouc (Cz)
Poznań	Posen	
Sieradz	Schieratz	
Siewierz		
Strzała	Strehla	
Strzelin	Strehlen	
Szczecin	Stettin	
Świecie	Schwetz	
Trzemeszno	Tremessen	
Ujście	Usch	
Włodzimierz		Vladimir-Volinsk (R)
Wolin	Wollin	
Wrocław	Breslau	Vratislav (Cz)
Wyszogród	Wiessegrad	

Provinces and Territories

Grody Czerwieńskie		Czerwien Territory (E)
Halicz [Księstwo Halickie]	Galizien	Galicia
Kujawy		Kujavia
Lubawa		Lubava
Łużyce	Nieder Lausitz	Lower Lusatia
Małopolska		Małopolska
Mazowsze		Mazovia
Milsko	Ober Lausitz	Upper Lusatia
Miśnia	Meissen	Meissen
Pomorze	Pommern	Pomerania
Rugia	Rügen	Rugia
Sandomierz		Sandomierz
Śląsk	Schlesien	Silesia
Uznam	Usedom	Uznam
Wołynia	Wolhynien	Volynia

Mountains

Rudawy	Erzgebirge
Sudety	Sudeten

Rivers

Bóbr	Bober	
Kwissa	Queiss	
Łaba	Elbe	
Noteć	Netze	
Odra	Oder	
Parsenta	Persante	
Trutina		Trutina (Cz)
Warta	Warthe	
Wisła	Weichsel	Vistula (E)

B

Slavic and Baltic Tribal Names

Polish	Text
Brzeżanie	Brzeżans
Bobrzanie	Bobrzans
Dziadoszanie	Dziadoszans
Jadźwingowie	Jadzwings
Kujawianie	Kujavians
Łęczycanie	Łęczycans
Licikawiki	Licikavians
Lubuszanie	Lubuszans
Lutici (Wieleci)	Luticians (Veletians)
Mazowszanie	Mazovians
Milczanie	Milczans
Obodryci	Obodrites
Opolanie	Opolans
Połanie	Polanie
Polabianie	Polabians
Pomorzanie	Pomeranians
Prusowie	Prussians
Radarowie	Radarians
Ranowie	Ranians
Stodoranie (Hawelanie)	Stodorans (Havelians)
Ślęzanie	Silesians
Wiślanie	Vistulans
Wolinianie	Wolinians

C

Royal Genealogies

Poland

Mieszko I	ca. 960–992
Bolesław Chrobry	992–1025
Mieszko II	1025–1034
Bezprym	1031
Interregnum	1034–1038
(Bolesław)	(1034–1037)
Kazimierz Odnowiciel	1038–1058
Bolesław Śmiały	1058–1079
Władysław Herman	1079–1102
Bolesław Krzywousty	1102–1138
Władysław Wygnaniec	1138–1146
Bolesław Kędzierzawy	1146–1173
Mieszko Stary	1173–1177
Kazimierz Sprawiedliwy	1177–1194

Bohemia

Václav	921–929 (d. 935)
Boleslav I	929 (935)–967
Boleslav II	967–999
Boleslav III	999–1002, 1003
Vladivoj	1002–1003
Bolesław Chrobry	1003–1004
Jaromír	1004–1012
Oldřich	1012–1034
Břetislav I	1034–1055

Spytihněv II	1055–1061
Vratislav II	1061–1092
Břetislav II	1092–1100
Bořivoj II	1100–1107 (coruler 1117–1120)
Svatopluk	1107–1109
Vladislav I	1109–1125
Soběslav I	1125–1140
Vladislav II	1140–1172
Bedřich	1172–1173
Soběslav II	1173–1180

Hungary

Géza	972–997
István I [Stephen I (E)]	997–1038
Peter Orseolo (the Venetian)	1038–1041, 1044–1046
Sámuel Aba	1041–1044
András	1046–1061
Béla I	1061–1063
Salamon	1063–1074
Géza I	1074–1077
László	1077–1095
Kálmán	1095–1114
István II	1114–1131
Béla II	1131–1141
Géza II	1141–1162
István III	1162–1172
Béla III	1172–1196

Kievan Rus

Sviatoslav	964–972
Jaropolk	972–978
Vladimir	978–1015
Sviatopolk	1015–1017, 1018–1019
Jaroslav Mudry	1017–1018, 1019–1054

Mstislav	1019–1035 (east of Dnieper)
Iziaslav	1054–1068, 1069–1073, 1076–1078
Sviatoslav	1073–1076
Vsevolod	1078–1093
Sviatopolk II	1093–1113
Vladimir Monomakh	1113–1125
Mstislav	1125–1132
Jaropolk	1132–1139
Vsevolod	1139–1146
Igor	1146
Iziaslav	1146–1154

Galicia

Volodimirko	1124–1152
Jaroslav Osmomysl	1152–1187
Oleg, Volodimir	1187–1188
Roman, András, Volodimir	1188–1199
Roman	1199–1205
Daniel	1205–1206

Holy Roman Emperors

Henry I (king of East Frankland)	918–936
Otto I (emperor from 963)	936–973
Otto II	973–983
Otto III	983–1002
Henry II	1002–1024
Conrad II	1024–1039
Henry III	1039–1056
Henry IV	1056–1106
Henry V	1106–1125
Lothar II	1125–1137
Conrad III	1138–1152
Frederick Barbarossa	1152–1190
Henry VI	1190–1197

D

Polish Historians

Manteuffel is indebted in his text to the Polish historians whose professional careers and major works are briefly outlined below. Although most of their writings have never been published in English, I have cited Polish titles in translation for the convenience of the reader.

Oswald Balzer (1858–1933). Law historian. One of the most prominent and influential historians of his period. Member of the faculty of the University of Lwów from 1887. His research was broad and varied, ranging from the medieval period to the nineteenth century, and included the formation and organization of the Piast state, legal history, and economics. His principal works include *Genealogy of the Piasts*, 1895; *Comparative History of the Slavic Law*, 1900; *The Polish Kingdom, 1295–1370*, 1920; *A Treatise on Kadłubek*, 1935; *Corpus Iuris Polonici*, vol. 3, 1906; vol. 4, 1910.

Karol Buczek (1902–). Curator of the Czartoryski Library in Kraków, 1930–1946. Member of the Institute of History in Warsaw, 1955–1972. His research focused on the economic, social, and state structure of early Piast Poland, the colonization process in East Central Europe, and historical cartography. His most important works include *Geographic Historical Foundations of East Prussia*, 1936; *Fairs and Cities under Polish Law*, 1964; *Polish Lands a Thousand Years Ago*, 1960; *The History of Polish Cartography from the 15th to the 18th Centuries*, 1966.

Roman Grodecki (1889–1964). Former member of the history faculty of the Jagiellonian University. He translated and annotated the Gall Anonim chronicle from Latin into Polish. He was the author of *The Beginnings of the "Vorwerk" in Poland, Piast Poland*, 1969. He was particularly concerned with economic history.

Marian Gumowski (1881–1974). Former director of the Emeryk Czapski-Hutten numismatical museum in Kraków, 1900–1909; then curator of the National Museum in Kraków, 1909–1919, before becoming director of the Wielkopolski Museum in Poznań, 1919–1932. He was editor of several periodicals pertaining to numismatics and museology. After World War II he joined the faculty of the University of Toruń, where he taught numismatics and ancient history. He was the author of some four hundred works pertaining particularly to numismatics, sphragistics, and heraldry. His classic work, *Handbook of Polish Numismatics* (1914), was translated into German in 1960.

Stanisław Kętrzyński (1876–1950). Member of the faculty of the University of Warsaw. Archivist and medievalist with special interest in the early Piast period and diplomatic history. He also served in the Polish diplomatic corps in Moscow (1925–1926) and at The Hague (1927–1931). He wrote numerous works on Gall Anonim, Saint Adalbert, Astryk Anastazy, and Kazimierz Odnowiciel. His classic work in diplomatic history was *A Survey of Polish Medieval Documents*, 1934. Contributed to the *Cambridge History of Poland*, 1950. Also interested in genealogy and sphragistics. Taught in underground university during Generalgouvernement; he was later arrested and placed in Auschwitz. Last published work was *Poland, Tenth and Eleventh Centuries*, 1961.

Stanisław Smolka (1854–1924). Member of the history faculty of the University of Lwów and later at the Jagiellonian University. Joined the Catholic University in Lublin after 1919. Medievalist. Principal works include *Henry the Bearded*, 1872; *Mieszko Stary and His Age*, 1881 (reprinted 1959); *Historical Sketches*, vol. 1, 1882; vol. 2, 1883; *Remarks on the Early Organization of the Piast State*, 1881.

Józef Widajewicz (1889–1954). Medievalist. Member of the history faculty at the University of Poznań before World War II;

after 1945 joined the Jagiellonian University. Principal studies include *Ibrahim ibn Jakub's Account of the Slavs*, 1946; *The Vistulan State*, 1947; *The Early Formation of Poland*, 1948. He also wrote studies on feudal services, obligations, and taxes.

Tadeusz Wojciechowski (1838–1919). Medievalist. Member of the history faculty at the University of Lwów, 1883–1907. Educated in Kraków and Vienna. Incarcerated for activities during Polish insurrection of 1860s. Main works pertained to analysis of primary sources and toponymic studies. Principal works include *Chrobotia: An Analysis of the Ancient Slavs*, vol. 1, 1873; *About Piast and the piast*, 1895; *The Polish Chronicles, Tenth to Fifteenth Centuries*, 1880; *Historical Sketches of the Eleventh Century*, 1904 (appeared in 1951 edition).

Zygmunt Wojciechowski (1900–1955). Member of the faculty of the University of Poznań from 1929. Work focused on legal history and the formation of the medieval Polish state. Principal works include *Studies on the Organization of the Polish State under the Piasts*, 1924; *The Political Structure of Silesia to the End of the Fourteenth Century*, 1932; *Poland along the Oder and the Vistula in the Tenth Century*, 1939; *The Polish State in the Middle Ages: A History of Its Structure*, 1945 (French translation, 1949).

Stanisław Zakrzewski (1873–1936). Professor of history at the University of Lwów from 1904. Studies often centered on the lives and activities of extraordinary historical figures. *Mieszko I*, 1925; *Bolesław Chrobry*, 1925.

Index

Entries are alphabetized according to the conventions of English, ignoring diacriticals.

Tadeusz Szoege-Manteuffel (1902–1970) represented an unshakable ethical and professional authority through his many roles in the Polish academic community after World War II. As archivist, professor of medieval studies at the University of Warsaw, director of the Institute of History, member of the Polish Academy of Sciences, and simply as a man of conscience and learning, he stood for the power of reason, balance, and tradition in postwar Polish scholarship.

Andrew Gorski, currently instructor in Polish for the Orchard Lake (Michigan) Schools was educated at Wayne State University (B.A., 1968), the University of Illinois, and the University of California at Berkeley (M.A., 1972). In 1974 he was awarded a Fulbright fellowship to Poland, and, in 1978, the Sendzimir Scholarship by the Kosciuszko Foundation. He is the author of a study of Baudelaire and Dostoevsky published in *Zagadnienia Rodzajów Literackich* and of several articles on topics pertaining to contemporary events in eastern Europe for the *Detroit News.* Paul W. Knoll is associate professor of history at the University of Southern California; his book *The Rise of the Polish Monarchy: Piast Poland in East Central Europe, 1320–1370* received the Kosciuszko Foundation Award in 1971.

The manuscript was edited by Sherwyn T. Carr. The maps were prepared by Karen Promo. The book was designed by Mary Primeau. The typeface for the text is Bembo, based on a design by Francisco Criffo about 1495. The display type is Camellia.

Manufactured in the United States of America